Jaime J. Sucher

Cocker Spaniels

Everything About Purchase, Care, Nutrition, Behavior, and Training

Filled with Full-color Photographs

BARRON'S

CONTENTS

WHAT IS A COCKER SPANIEL?

Dogs are considered the first domesticated animals. The actual domestication process, however, is hard to trace because it is impossible for archaeologists to distinguish tame wolves from early domestic dogs. Nevertheless, the earliest indisputable records of "dog" remains, date back some 12,000 years.

Humans and Dogs

Wolves

The relationship that began with taming the wolf most likely came about as a result of the hunting and scavenging practices of both humans and wolves. Wolves probably started attaching themselves to camps of human hunters, scavenging meals wherever they could. It is also possible that humans learned group hunting techniques by observing how the wolf pack hunts.

At first, people probably killed any wolf that ventured too close to their camps. However, in time the humans could provide enough food for both themselves and their attached pack of wolves. Eventually the newborn wolf pups began to rely on their human "masters" for food, and later for shelter.

While the exact time sequences are unknown, over the next 10,000 years people began to take control of the breeding practices of their "dogs." Particular characteristics were chosen for inbreeding and, as a result, the variations between the different types of dogs became more pronounced. The larger and more aggressive animals may have been bred together to create a progeny of "watchdogs." The more placid or submissive animals may have been mated to supply dogs that would aid in locating and stalking game.

By the first century A.D. the Romans had written records that contained advice on breeding dogs. They classified dogs into six different groups: house guardian dogs, shepherd dogs, sporting dogs, fighting or war dogs, dogs that ran by scent, and swift dogs that ran by sight. Most modern dogs have ancestors from one or more of these six classifications. It is unlikely, however, that any modern breed resembles the dogs of ancient Rome. Only within the past 100 years, has the growing knowledge of genetics allowed us to increase the diversity of breeds while establishing pure bloodlines at the same time. Nevertheless, despite the differences in appearance and temperament, all modern dogs still possess many basic instincts that humans were never able to breed out of the wolf.

Origins and Early History

Spaniels

The spaniel comprises a very large family of dogs and has a long history. While the dog's exact origins are unknown, a "spaynel" or "spanyell" is mentioned in some writings of the fourteenth century. Although also found in France and Switzerland, spaniels are commonly believed to have originated in Spain.

It was not until their introduction into England that most of the spaniel breeds we know today began to take shape. The English breeders mated these dogs rather indiscriminately at first, with the size of the dog being the only criterion for selection. The initial step in the separation of breeds was to divide the animals into land spaniels and water spaniels. The large, curly coated dogs were placed in the water spaniel group, while all of the rest were considered land spaniels. Later, the land spaniels were further separated into groups, with size again being the only criterion.

The Spaniel Breeds Today

Today there are nine spaniel breeds in the sporting dog group: American Water, Clumber, Cocker, English Cocker, English Springer, Field, Irish Water, Sussex, and Welsh Springer.

In the early 1800s, two types of English spaniels gained rapidly in popularity. One was the liver and white "springing spaniel," obviously the ancestor of today's modern English Springer Spaniel. The other was, as one breeder wrote, "smaller with a more curly type of coat and feathering, and diverse in color." This dog became known as the "cocking spaniel" because it was very proficient at hunting woodcock.

During this period, when only size separated the various classifications, it was possible to get a Cocker, a Field, and a Springer Spaniel all from the same litter. However, as dog shows came into being, the characteristics of each spaniel strain became more refined. Nevertheless, up until the 1870s, the only qualification for a dog to compete as a Cocker was that it weigh less than 25 pounds (11.3 kg).

Cockers were originally designated as the group of smallest spaniels, but this classification also included the very small, or Toy Spaniel. Since true Cockers and Toy Spaniels were bred for entirely different purposes, these two groups were separated. The English Toy Spaniels were bred as companion animals, while the Cockers maintained their status as sporting dogs.

Finally, in 1892, the Cocker Spaniel was recognized as a separate and distinct breed by the Kennel Club of England. There was still, however, one more change to come.

In 1879 the most famous of all Cockers was born. His name was Obo, and he was the offspring of a Sussex Spaniel sire (father) and a Field Spaniel dam (mother). Obo was bred to a female Cocker, which was taken to Canada while she was in whelp. Their son, Obo II, was then sold to a breeder in New Hampshire. Obo II was a black dog with a curly coat, especially on the shoulders and hindquarters, which also had profuse feathering. Obo II weighed 23½ pounds (10.7 kg), and he measured 9½ inches (24 cm) from foot to withers. This dog proved to be the grandfather of all modern Cockers. He was a direct ancestor of a Cocker named Robinhurst Foreglow, and all winning Cocker Spaniels past and present are direct descendants of Foreglow. All other Cocker lines have completely disappeared from the breed over the years.

To satisfy the needs of a growing number of breeders on this continent, the American Spaniel Club (ASC) was formed in 1881. Nevertheless, there was still a certain amount of interbreeding between the Cocker Spaniels in England and those in the United States and Canada.

In 1935 the English Cocker Spaniel Club of America (ECSCA) was formed, not so much to promote the breed as to discourage the wanton interbreeding of the two varieties and to prevent their being shown against each other. Up until this time, the English Cocker had been recognized as a variety of Cocker but not as a different breed. One can imagine the confusion that must have occurred when the same set of criteria was used to judge two different types of Cocker Spaniels.

Through extensive research into the pedigrees of English Cocker Spaniels, the ECSCA was able to ensure that the registered dogs had no mixture of American bloodlines. This research was completed in 1941, and five years later the American Kennel Club (AKC) recognized the English Cocker Spaniel as a separate breed, the American, or what is now called simply the Cocker Spaniel.

Since 1946 the ASC has had the responsibility of maintaining the integrity of the modern Cocker Spaniel, and has helped many Cocker breeders through its establishment of the breed standard. The standard is a written description of Cocker Spaniels by which they are judged at dog shows.

Characteristics of the Breed

The following is an interpretation of the AKC-approved Standard for the Cocker Spaniel, which describes in writing the physical characteristics and temperament of the perfect Cocker. It provides all the criteria by which the appearance and behavior of the dog can be measured objectively. While reading this section, you should refer to the pictures and diagrams in this book. These illustrations will make it easier for you to learn about the Cocker's anatomy.

General Appearance

As the smallest member of the sporting dog group, the Cocker should be of ideal size and well balanced, with a compact and sturdy body. The Cocker's head must be "cleanly chiseled and refined." When standing still, the Cocker holds his head and forequarters high on muscular shoulders, while keeping his forelegs straight and perpendicular to the ground. His back will slope down slightly toward the strong and muscular hindquarters.

Despite his small size the Cocker is capable of considerable speed and has great endurance. Most importantly, however, the standard emphasizes that the dog must be "free and merry, sound, well balanced throughout, and in action show a keen inclination to work." The Cocker's temperament should be calm and steady with no hint of shyness or fear.

Head and Facial Features

The head must be well proportioned and in balance with the rest of the body. To fulfill this image of balance, the distance from the tip of the nose to the stop (the sloped area between the forehead and the muzzle) is half the distance from the stop, up and over the head, to the base of the skull. The Cocker possesses a well-rounded skull. The stop should be steeply sloped, well pronounced, and positioned between well-defined eyebrows. The bony structure below the eyes is clear-cut yet blends smoothly into the dog's cheeks.

The muzzle must appear square and be proportionately wide and long, with the upper and lower jaw of equal length. The upper lips are pendulous and hang down enough to cover the lower jaw. The teeth must be strong, sound, and meet in a "scissors bite."

The Cocker's nose must be of a size proportional to the muzzle and face. It must be black in color for black and for black and tan Cockers. Liver and white dogs may have brown noses, but the darker the better. The nose color should match the color of the eye rim. Because the Cocker is a sporting dog that relies on its nose, the nostrils should be well defined.

The eyes, which are an important physical feature of the Cocker Spaniel, should convey an "intelligent, alert, soft, and appealing" expression. This expression is attained through proper eye color, size, and position. The eyes should be large and positioned to look straight ahead. The eyeballs must be round and full and set behind almond-shaped rims. The iris should be dark brown in color.

The size and shape of the Cocker's ears are very important because they add to the overall character of this breed. They should begin no higher than a point even with the lower part of the eye. They should be "wide, long, and oval in shape," "of fine leather," and "well feathered." When the ears are pulled forward, the ends should reach the tip of the dog's nose.

Neck and Shoulders

The neck must be long enough to allow the dog to easily sniff the ground, an important feature for any hunting dog. It should also be well muscled, and the throat should be straight and void of loose-hanging skin. The neck should taper slightly as it moves from shoulders to head and should also arch slightly.

The shoulders should be set well back, at an angle perpendicular to the upper arm. This angle allows for free movement of the forelegs and a long stride. The shoulders should be sloping, well defined, and smooth and free of protruding joints. The angle of the upper points of the shoulders (the withers) should allow "a wide spring of rib."

Overall Body Appearance

The Cocker's body is small, compact, and sturdy and gives the impression of strength. The distance from the withers to the ground is about 2 inches (5.08 cm), more than the body length from the withers to the base of the tail.

The back is strong and evenly sloped down toward the tail. The hips are wide, and the haunches are well rounded and muscular. The chest is deep, and the "well-sprung ribs" must come to a position lower than the dog's elbows. The rib cage must be large enough to house the heart and lungs adequately, yet it must not interfere with the movement of the forelegs.

The Cocker possesses a docked (cut) tail, which is carried in a line continuous with the slope line of the back (or slightly higher). When the dog is at work, its tail should wag incessantly, reflecting its merry as well as industrious temperament.

The forelegs must be strongly boned, muscular, and held parallel to each other, and straight. The side view should show the elbows directly below the withers. The pasterns (the equivalent of human forearms) are short and strong. The hind legs are also well boned and muscular. The stifle (the equivalent of a knee) should have "good angulation," and the Cocker must possess strong, powerful thighs. The hocks (the points where the lower legs join with the feet) are strong and low set, and are parallel when viewed from behind. The feet, large, round, and firm with "horny pads," should turn neither in nor out. All dewclaws can be removed.

Coat

The Cocker's body coat is of medium length and is dense enough to provide protection from the elements, while his head hairs are short and fine. Ample feathering should appear on the dog's ears, legs, abdomen, and chest but should not hide the Cocker's true features or movement.

The standard also states that the texture of the dog's coat is extremely important. "The coat is silky, flat or slightly wavy, and of a texture which permits easy care." The coat should not be too wavy or curly or "cottony" textured.

Color and Markings

Cocker Spaniels vary greatly in color, and thus each variety has its own acceptable standards.

The black variety is jet black with little or no shadings of brown or liver. Small amounts of white on chest or throat are penalized. All other white markings disqualify the dog from bench competitions.

Any solid color other than black must be a uniform shade, with lighter-colored feathering acceptable. White markings are dealt with in the same way as for the black variety.

Black and tans have definite tan markings on jet black bodies. The markings must be distinct and plainly visible, and can range in color from light cream to darkest red. The markings are restricted in amount to 10 percent or less of the body area; more extensive markings result in disqualification. Tan markings that are not easily visible, or a lack of markings in any of the following locations, will disqualify the dog:

1. Over the eye

2. On the sides of the muzzle and on the cheeks

3. On the undersides of the ears

4. On all feet and legs

5. Under the tail

The presence or absence of marking on the chest is not penalized. Tan on the muzzle that extends upward over the snout will be penalized. White markings will result in penalties or disqualifications as in the solid varieties.

Particolored varieties have "two or more definite colors appearing in clearly defined markings, distinctly distributed over the body."

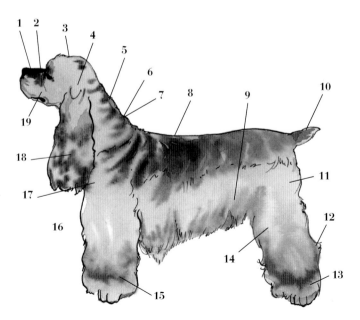

Exterior anatomy of the Cocker Spaniel
 1. *muzzle*
 2. *stop*
 3. *skull*
 4. *ear*
 5. *neckline*
 6. *withers*
 7. *shoulder*
 8. *rib cage*
 9. *loin*
 10. *docked tail*
 11. *hindquarters*
 12. *hock*
 13. *rear pastern*
 14. *stifle*
 15. *front pastern*
 16. *forequarters*
 17. *brisket*
 18. *chest*
 19. *cheek*

Disqualification will result if the primary color covers 90 percent of the dog. Secondary colors that are limited to a single location on the body also disqualify the dog. The particolor variety includes the Cockers that are commonly referred to as roans or tricolors.

Movement

The following is taken directly from the AKC Standard, which I consider the best description possible:

"The Cocker Spaniel, though the smallest of the sporting dogs, possesses a typical sporting dog gait. Prerequisite to good movement is balance between the front and rear assemblies. He drives with his strong, powerful rear quarters and is properly constructed in the shoulders and forelegs so that he can reach forward without constriction in a full stride to counterbalance the driving force from the rear. Above all, his gait is coordinated, smooth, and effortless. The dog must cover ground with his action and excessive animation should never be mistaken for proper gait."

Height

The ideal height at the withers is 15 inches (38 cm) for a male and 14 inches (35.6 cm) for a female Cocker. Height variation can be no greater than 1/2 inch (1.4 cm) above and below the ideal. A Cocker of excessive height will be disqualified; insufficient height incurs a penalty.

Cocker Spaniel Differences

Although the differences between the American and the English Cocker are quite obvious to the show judge, they are not always clear to the novice. While the English Cocker is slightly

larger than its American counterpart, the most obvious difference can be seen in the head shapes. Compared to the English dog, the American Cocker has a distinctly domed skull, as well as a deep pronounced stop and more clearly defined eyebrows. Also, the American dog's lips tend to hang down farther and more loosely, and its eyes are slightly larger and set more to look straight ahead than those of the English Cocker Spaniel. Finally, the American Cocker carries a much more profuse coat than its English cousin.

IS THE COCKER SPANIEL THE DOG FOR ME?

The Cocker Spaniel's history as a "gundog" has had a great influence on its temperament and personality. Cockers are highly intelligent and therefore relatively easy to train. They are a bright, sturdy, and loyal breed with an assertive yet stable personality.

Making Intelligent Choices

Cocker Spaniels also possess an innate sensitivity to the moods of their masters. These traits make the Cocker an ideal dog for the first-time owner. In addition, the Cocker Spaniel's ability to adapt readily to the role of family companion makes it a wonderful addition to a family with small children. These qualities, combined with the pure beauty of the breed and the wide variety of colors available, provide some explanation of why the Cocker Spaniel has become one of the most popular dogs of our time.

While owning a dog may seem completely natural, it must be pointed out that not every breed of dog is right for every type of human lifestyle. In fact, there are certain lifestyles that are not suitable for any breed of dog. It is vital to both the physical and mental health of a dog that the animal be given a suitable home and the attention it needs to form a proper bond with its master.

Attributes and Needs

For all its fine attributes, the Cocker may not be the ideal pet for everyone. The Cocker Spaniel is a long-haired breed and requires frequent grooming to keep her coat in top condition. The same thick coat that is designed to protect the dog from the elements will also collect dirt and mud. Another disadvantage to owning a long-haired dog is that, when she sheds, it leaves long hairs all over the carpet and furniture. This is something to keep in mind, especially if you or anyone else in your family suffers from allergies.

Being a hunting breed, the Cocker Spaniel needs to be kept in peak physical condition. Beneath its soft, dense coat lies a rugged, muscular, and powerful body. To maintain its muscle tone and mental sharpness, the Cocker needs adequate exercise. While this breed is small enough to adapt to virtually any housing arrangement, you will need to have a place where you can bring your dog for its regular workout.

While the Cocker will easily adapt to any lifestyle that keeps her close to her master, she is at her best when she is tramping through the woods or romping through the park, following her keen sense of smell as she bounds from one adventure to another. The Cocker Spaniel requires a constant challenge to keep her mentally sharp; when she is kept in this condition, there are few breeds that can compare.

All of the traits mentioned in this section are latent in every Cocker. It is up to the owner, however, to bring them to the surface so that they become a dominant part of the dog's personality. Bringing out the best your Cocker has to offer will take time, energy, patience, and understanding.

Factors to Consider Before Purchasing

Whether or not to buy a dog is an important decision. Many people are not aware, at the time of purchase, of the responsibilities of dog ownership. To buy a dog impulsively is an irre-sponsible act and often leads to an unhappy relationship for both the dog and its owner.

Purchasing a dog should never be a "spur of the moment" decision. Rather, to buy or not to buy must be thought through in a careful and sensible fashion.

If you have any additional questions about owning a Cocker, you should contact a local chapter of the ASC. This organization can supply you with detailed answers to all your inquiries, as well as with a list of reputable breeders in your area whom you can visit before you make your decision.

But then, when you have decided that you want to own a dog and that the Cocker Spaniel is the right breed for you—wouldn't you know it, there are more choices to be made!

A Puppy or an Adult?

Speaking as someone who has endured the experience, I honestly believe that there is no greater satisfaction in dog ownership than acquiring a tiny, fragile, adorable, eight-week-old ball of fur and energy, and raising it to be an obedient, loyal, and loving companion. Notice, however, that I used the term "endured."

Purchasing a Puppy

Let it be known at the outset that raising puppies is not always a bowl of cherries, especially for the novice. House-training alone can become, quite literally, a nightmare if it is not done correctly. There may be additional problems as well, not the least of which is the teething puppy. Personally, I feel that, when you weigh the pros and cons of raising a puppy, the pros win by a landslide, but in truth, the experience is not for everyone.

Cocker Spaniel puppies are playful, intelligent, and adventurous little creatures, and with the proper training techniques you can use these qualities to your advantage. By making training sessions resemble a game, you can teach a Cocker puppy an incredible number of commands or tricks—and your dog will love you all the more for the lessons.

There are other advantages to raising a dog from puppyhood. If you have older children, raising a puppy is a great way to bring the family together and to teach the kids the responsibilities of pet ownership. Moreover, starting with a puppy will allow you to "mold" the dog to suit your personal or family lifestyle. Purchasing an eight-week-old puppy for a toddler, however, could be counterproductive. By the time the child is old enough to truly appreciate her, the dog would be several years old and already set in her ways.

Another benefit to raising a puppy is the satisfaction you will get from a job well done. You will experience this satisfaction each and every time your Cocker fetches her stick and releases it into your hand, or when the dog comes eagerly when you call her name or stops on a dime when you tell her to halt. Truly, the best way to obtain a well-trained pet is to train her yourself.

While raising a puppy properly may sound simple, do not kid yourself. To bring out the best a puppy has to offer takes time, patience, energy, and dedication. If you work diligently with a Cocker puppy, you will eventually be rewarded with a loyal and loving companion. However, if you are lax in your training, you will probably end up with an unruly dog—a situation that is not very good for either owner or animal.

Considerations Before Buying

1 Keep in mind that owning a dog is a long-term commitment. A Cocker may live for a dozen years, and with recent advances in animal nutrition and health care, the average life span of the breed will only increase.

2 Be aware that a great deal of time, energy, and patience are required to raise, train, and properly care for a Cocker Spaniel. While this breed is renowned for its ability to learn, training requires a strict regimen in order to optimize your dog's performance. In addition, your dog will require daily walks and grooming.

Should you decide to purchase a Cocker puppy, you must be willing to rearrange your daily schedule to meet the dog's needs. Puppies must be watched much more carefully than adult dogs, and they require several small feedings each day.

3 Whether you are looking for a puppy or an adult dog, you will have to make plans for housing your pet both indoors and out. If you do not have a large yard, you will need access to a park or woods where you can take your dog for exercise. If you have a suitable yard, you may have to build a fence or a run to prevent your dog from straying.

4 Owning a Cocker brings additional expenses. Besides the initial price of the dog (see page 21), there is the cost of equipment such as bowls, leashes, collars, and brushes. Food may cost as much as $30 per month. There will be license and registration fees, veterinarian's bills, and incidental expenses such as the cost of building a fence or run in your yard.

Consider working with a Cocker Spaniel rescue organization. These nonprofit groups, are dedicated to finding families that can provide a caring, loving home to abandoned, abused, or unwanted dogs. Rescue groups can be found on the Internet, or through the local humane society.

These organizations are a great source of information, and can provide sound advice before, during, and after an adoption. They will also make sure that all dogs that they put up for adoption are up-to-date on vaccinations, and are spayed or neutered (if old enough). Rescue groups are committed to finding the right match for their dogs, so you have a much better chance of getting a dog that is right for your lifestyle. As these organizations are not always privy to the history of the dog, they take extra time to understand a dog's temperament, and match it to prospective owners who are prepared for it. In this way they spend more time finding the right home for their dogs, and less going through the rescue process a second time.

Acquiring an Older Dog

With these facts in mind, one can easily see the advantages of getting an adult dog. A well-trained adult Cocker Spaniel makes a wonderful pet, especially for those who do not have the time or the desire to train a puppy. A house-trained adult makes a marvelous companion for the elderly, for she requires little supervision.

Also, a well-adjusted adult Cocker will have little trouble acclimating itself to a new owner and environment. As long as these dogs get the love and attention they need, they will usually make the change without a hitch.

The greatest drawback to owning an older Cocker is that you may find it difficult to break the dog of any bad habits it has already acquired. While this book contains some tips on teaching an old dog new tricks, be warned in advance that the lessons are not easy.

Selecting a Show Dog

If, in obtaining a dog, you have the express intent of showing her in the ring, there are basically two options. The first is to select a puppy based on her parents' pedigree and to raise it yourself. In this case you will have the advantage of self-satisfaction at your achievement, and you will also encounter less expense. However, there is always the chance that a late-arising fault in the puppy may ruin your ring hopes. The other option is to purchase a mature show dog, for which you will be expected to pay significantly more. This second option, of course, assures you of getting the quality and beauty of a ring dog.

A Male or a Female?

If you are getting a Cocker strictly as a companion animal, there are a few differences between the sexes you may wish to consider. Female Cockers tend to be slightly smaller, slightly more sedate, and at times a little more affectionate and sensitive than their male counterparts, which are sometimes a bit more independent. However, these differences may not even be noticeable unless you own both a male and a female at the same time.

The choice of sex is much more important should you plan on becoming a breeder. If you are considering starting a kennel, then, of course, you will want to get a female, so that you can breed her to obtain your stock.

There are an alarming number of homeless dogs in the United States because of the irresponsibility of many dog owners, and steps need to be taken to prevent the proliferation of unwanted animals. Regardless of sex, if you are getting a Cocker strictly as a companion animal, and not planning to enter conformation shows however, neutered dogs would be disqualified). Females can be spayed between five and six months of age, just prior to their first heat. Male dogs, that reach sexual maturity about six months of age, can be neutered as early as three months. Spaying and neutering also provide many health benefits. Neutered dogs cannot contract an infection or cancer of the testes, and the risk of prostate problems is greatly reduced. For females, spaying reduces the risk of ovarian cysts, breast tumors, and false pregnancies.

How to Buy a Cocker Spaniel

If you wish to buy a high-quality Cocker Spaniel, it is of the utmost importance that you deal with a well-established and reputable source. A quality dog comes from good breeding stock, has been well cared for, and is healthy and free of the genetic ailments that plague some breeds. You can get a list of reliable Cocker Spaniel breeders in your area from the AKC or from the secretary of the ASC. Be

aware, however, that while it is more convenient to obtain a Cocker from a local breeder, traveling the extra distance to visit as many breeders as possible sometimes pays dividends.

Reputable Sources

Start by making appointments with all of the breeders on your list. The objective, while visiting each facility, is to inspect both the dogs and their housing. Reliable breeders are very proud of their stock, so do not be afraid to ask questions. These people understand that the quality of their Cockers is a direct reflection of their concern for their dogs and the care they give them. A conscientious breeder will make every effort to answer your inquiries, as they want to make sure that their dogs find safe homes and caring masters.

Like many other breeds, Cocker Spaniels are subject to certain hereditary ailments. A reputable breeder, however, will never breed any dog known to carry one of these defects. Ask the breeders you visit if their dogs have been checked and cleared of genetically linked diseases.

Ask if the medical history of their breeding stock is in the Canine Health Information Center (CHIC) database. CHIC is jointly sponsored by the AKC and the Orthopedic Foundation for Animals (OFA). Its goal is to provide a source of health information for owners, breeders, and scientists to assist in the breeding of healthy dogs. The CHIC database for Cockers presently includes the results of eye clearance tests by the Canine Eye Registry Foundation (CERF) and the results of OFA evaluations for hip dysplasia. CHIC is also presently working on a DNA database, which they hope will lead to the discovery of the genetic links for other canine hereditary ailments. If the breeder does have

his or her dogs listed, the results can be reviewed online at *www.caninehealthinfo.org*. If the breeder does not have his or her dogs' test results in the database, then you should ask why. Finally, be sure the dogs have been tested for von Willebrand's disease, which affects blood-clotting ability. (A more detailed discussion of hereditary ailments is given in the chapter entitled "Ailments and Illnesses.")

While visiting each breeder, check the conditions under which the Cocker Spaniels are kept. Make sure that the facilities are spacious and clean. Look at the adult Cockers to make sure that all of the breeding stock is happy and healthy. These dogs should be clean and have thick, shiny coats, and should exhibit the sturdiness, balance, and happy, attentive temperament that typifies this breed.

Only after you have questioned the breeder and inspected the kennels and the adult dogs should you look at the puppies. Many a potential Cocker owner has made the mistake of going into a breeder's kennel and running straight off to see the puppies. Be warned that it is extremely hard to form an objective opinion as to the quality of the breeder when you are enthralled by the antics of these dark-eyed, floppy-eared fluff balls. Stay cool! Try to remember that, while all Cocker puppies are adorable, there is more to this breed than just outward appearances.

Avoid the Impulse Purchase

Avoid buying a puppy impulsively. Be sure to check out each and every breeder on your list. Remember that the time you spend finding a physically healthy and well-adjusted puppy will save you a lot of anguish later on. By the same token, never be tempted to buy a Cocker Spaniel on the basis of price. There are usually very good reasons why some dogs are less expensive. A lower price usually indicates that the dog was bred strictly for profit by an inexperienced breeder, or that she is in poor health. The extra money you spend for a high-quality dog at the time of purchase is often less than the additional veterinary bills that a low-priced puppy will incur.

Once you have confidence in the quality of the breeder, it is time to consider which one of the puppies you will take home to its new family.

Selecting the Right Puppy

As you are aware, Cockers come in a wide variety of color patterns, including solid colors (black, red, cream, buff, and liver) as well as particolors (black and white, black and tan, and a few liver and whites) and even a tricolor (black, white, and tan). Although color may influence your choice of a puppy, it should

never be your primary concern. There are more important factors you need to consider.

✔ Make sure that all of the puppies in the litter are healthy. Their coats should be smooth and shiny.

✔ Now check the puppy you have in mind to buy. Examine her eyes and ears, making sure that they are not running or have any signs of discharge. The eyes should be bright and have a friendly expression. Examine the nose to make sure it is not running. The nose of a healthy Cocker puppy is usually wet, but a dry nose does not always indicate illness. Check the teeth and gums for unusual bleeding.

✔ Then look critically at the puppy's physical build. While Cocker puppies are small, they should still appear to be sturdy, rugged little creatures.

✔ Finally, observe the puppy's temperament. A Cocker Spaniel puppy should be friendly, alert, eager, and curious. Her tail should be wagging, and there should be no sign of either aggression or extreme shyness. Cockers are hunting dogs and as such should never be unfriendly toward, or afraid of, unthreatening people.

Temperament

Another good indicator of the puppy's temperament is the behavior of its mother. After all, much of the puppy's physical and behavioral traits are inherited from her parents. Watch how the mother reacts with the breeder. She should exhibit all of the behavioral traits that characterize this hunting breed. The mother should appear eager to please her master and show no signs of fear of people.

A final note on selecting a puppy: It is always a good idea to choose a puppy with a temperament that will suit your lifestyle. As I have already mentioned, all Cocker puppies are cute and cuddly. However, if you watch the litter very carefully, you will begin to see subtle differences from one puppy to the next. While watching the puppies play together, you will notice which ones are bolder and which are more submissive. If you have an active family lifestyle or have children, you may want to choose a livelier or bolder puppy that will not be intimidated by a hubbub of human activity. If you lead a quiet life, then perhaps a calmer and more sedate puppy is for you.

Pedigree, Health Record, and Breeder's Contract

A pedigree is a written record of a dog's recent ancestry, and has special notations marking all AKC show champions within the family tree. While a pedigree with many championship notations is impressive, you should give most of your attention to the dogs that precede the puppy by one or two generations. If all seems satisfactory, ask for a copy of the puppy's medical records. Your veterinarian will need to know when the puppy was last vaccinated and wormed. You will likely also need to review and sign a breeder contract, which expressly states all of the guarantees associated with the sale. As the buyer, make sure that all agreements previously given verbally are in writing. This can be done by adding a written amendment to the breeder's standard contract. Make sure that you can live up to all of the conditions and requirements listed in the contract, and are aware of stated consequences for not meeting them.

If you are buying a show or hunting dog, be sure it is stated as such in the contract, and that the puppy is not identified as a "companion pet." In most cases a puppy contract will contain disclaimers stating that a puppy is being sold as a "prospect." This is normal. While conscientious breeders do their best to make sure their dogs represent the ideal Cocker, they cannot guarantee a puppy will grow up with the perfect overbite, or that the environment at the new owner's home will not adversely affect its temperament. As the buyer, however, you will want written guarantees should the dog have serious physical or behavioral problems. So before you sign any contract, be sure to discuss your expectations with the breeder, and include written amendments for all contract points that require clarification.

How Much Will the Dog Cost?

While the initial purchase price of a Cocker Spaniel will vary, you should expect to spend at least $250. Show-quality puppies from champion-caliber lineage may sell for as much as $1,000. In general, the better the bloodlines, the higher the cost. Likewise, the older a puppy, the more expensive she will be because the breeder has invested more time and money in her.

People often wonder why well-raised purebred dogs are so expensive. The answer is quite simple. As you have already learned, the Cocker Spaniel, like other purebreds, has a special place in history and culture. She also has certain physical and mental characteristics that make the breed unique. Keeping and raising a purebred requires care that goes far beyond basic food and shelter. It is the breeder's objective to "create" the perfect dog, and this requires skill, time, patience, education, and, of course, a proven track record. If one considers only a reasonable hourly wage for the time breeders

spend on their dogs, it is evident that these "expensive" dogs are really sold at bargain prices. The warning bears repetition: Beware of "cheap" dogs. The old adage "You get what you pay for" is all too true when buying a dog.

The Costs of Ownership

As stated earlier, food for your Cocker may cost as much as $30 a month, and there are also licensing fees, for which you should check with your local town hall or animal shelter. You will also need to purchase certain equipment for feeding, housing, and grooming your Cocker.

Veterinarian costs must also be considered. A Cocker will require immunizations and check-ups to ensure its ongoing health. Your pet may have to be wormed. If your puppy should become sick or be injured, additional, perhaps costly, medical treatment may be needed.

Finally, you will have to pay a fee to register your dog with the American Kennel Club, and there are annual dues if you join the American Spaniel Club. Should you decide to either show or breed your dog, the process can become truly expensive. In summary, the costs involved in owning a Cocker Spaniel go far beyond the initial purchase price.

A final note on the cost of quality puppies: Keep in mind that you are spending a reasonable amount to ensure that your Cocker is healthy and sound and is a proud representative of its breed. But, in truth, the dog does not know how much money you paid for her, nor does she care. If you start with a quality puppy, and give her the care, attention, and affection she needs, she will freely give back to you all of her love and loyalty. What a priceless dividend on your investment!

HOUSING AND SUPPLIES

The Cocker does not require as large an area as do bigger breeds. Your dog's indoor territory will consist of its feeding and sleeping areas, which offer a refuge where it can eat in peace and rest whenever the need arises.

House Dog Requirements

The Feeding and Sleeping Areas

To help your Cocker feel secure, you should place his bed in a room that is not subject to heavy human traffic, but in which the dog will not be isolated from contact with people. It is also advisable to choose a room where the dog can easily be confined when you go to bed or leave the house. In locating the bed, a corner of the room is preferred because the dog is then protected on two sides, adding to its sense of security. You should avoid placing the bed in direct sunlight or in a drafty location.

Your Cocker's feeding area should also provide a sense of security, and therefore you can follow the same rules used to select a sleeping area. It is recommended, however, that you feed your dog in a room that can be easily cleaned, such as the kitchen. It is vitally important that your Cocker be left in peace in its eating area. Nervous dogs have trouble digesting food properly, and this difficulty will eventually lead to other biological problems, which can be quite messy.

Take time and use thought in selecting your Cocker's eating and sleeping areas so that they will not have to be changed later on. Your dog will not feel comfortable or secure if it must constantly search for a quiet place to sleep or eat. Permanent and peaceful sleeping and eating areas will help prevent undue stress on your Cocker and allow you to avoid the physical and behavioral problems associated with a tense, unhappy animal.

Once you have decided where your dog will sleep, you must choose a type of bed. Dogs are "denning animals," and feel much more secure in the confined, well-protected space of a cage or crate than an open sleeping box. A crate/cage will quickly become your Cocker's "home" and he will seek it out, voluntarily, whenever he feels the need to rest. I recommend using a fiberglass shipping crate. Not only will the crate provide shelter, it can also serve a functional purpose in house-training, raising, and training your Cocker. These crates can be easily taken apart to clean, are relatively draft free, are easily moved, can be used

for traveling, and do not have bars reaching from floor to top, which makes them very safe for puppies at any age. The appropriate size crate for a Cocker Spaniel should be approximately 20 inches (50 cm) high by 24 inches (61 cm) wide by 30 inches (76 cm) long.

You can also consider using a full wire cage, but you should be aware that a puppy's tiny teeth and toes can sometimes be trapped between the bars of some cages. The cage should have the same dimensions as described

for a travel crate, but be sure the bars are welded close enough together to prevent a puppy's muzzle and paws from squeezing through and getting caught. If you buy the full cage, you will also need to buy or make a fabric cover that will allow access to the front entry, but will cover the remaining sides of the cage in order to prevent drafts.

If you decide not to use a cage, purchase a sleeping box or a sleeping basket (the latter may offer your dog some added security) big enough to accommodate a spread-out adult Cocker. If you build your own sleeping box, use only non-splintering hardwoods and make sure that the box allows easy access to your puppy or adult Cocker. Because many paints and stains can be toxic, leave the box unfinished.

If you have a puppy, you should line the bottom of his sleeping quarters with plastic or an old piece of linoleum, covered with a good layer of cedar shavings or shredded newspapers topped with an old blanket. This will provide your dog with a very comfortable bed that can be easily cleaned or disposed of in case of "accidents."

Outdoor Needs

Being originally bred for hunting, the Cocker Spaniel has little trouble adapting to life outdoors. His coat is perfectly designed to protect him from the elements, keep him warm in the colder weather, and prevent him from overheating in the summer. Cockers are at their best when they are outdoors and have some room to roam, and many Cocker owners appreciate the fact that they can keep their dogs outside when they are away from home.

If you decide to keep your dog outside while you are away, you must be sure that he cannot escape your property. If your yard is not adequately fenced, you must provide your Cocker with a run. The run should be at least 4 feet (1.3 m) wide by 12 feet (4 m) long by 6 feet (2 m) high and enclosed by a chain link fence. While the height of the fence may seem excessive for a Cocker, remember that the fence also serves to keep other animals away from your pet. You can run a concrete footer or place cinder blocks tightly around the base to prevent the dog from digging under the fence. Do not bury boards to keep a chewing or digging Cocker in his run. Boards can splinter and rot and become a liability instead of a safety measure.

The bottom of the run should be covered with a few inches of smooth stone to provide drainage and to prevent the ground from becoming muddy. Avoid using a concrete base, which will retain the smell of urine. It is also very important that a portion of the run provides your dog with shade and protection from the elements.

A properly constructed doghouse is the best form of outdoor shelter. The floor should be raised several inches above the ground in order to keep the house dry and prevent invasion from insects. The dimensions must be large enough to comfortably accommodate a stretched-out adult dog, yet not so large that during cold weather the space cannot be heated with warmth from the dog's body. A Cocker Spaniel requires a shelter that has the same dimensions as its cage.

Whether you choose to buy a doghouse or to build it yourself, there are additional features that you may want to consider. A hinged roof

This doghouse is cleverly designed with a hinged lid for easy cleaning and a layout that offers added protection from the elements.

will give you better access and make cleaning much easier. The opening should be covered with a flap of canvas or a blanket to keep out the wind and rain; and if you live in a cold climate, the doghouse should be fully insulated. When positioning the structure, have the opening face south, out of the cold north winds.

To facilitate cleaning the shelter, I recommend lining the floor with a piece of linoleum or another easy-to-clean material. Then add a layer of cedar shavings, and cover it with an old blanket.

Regardless of how well insulated or weather-proof your doghouse is, I do not recommend keeping your pet outdoors during cold weather for a long period of time.

Additional Equipment

Food and Water Dishes

If dogs could talk, I am sure that they would say that the most important items of equipment you should get for them are food and water dishes, preferably ones that are sturdy and non-breakable. While bowls are available in plastic and ceramics, stainless steel is a preferable material. Plastic bowls may leach chemicals into a dog's drinking water, which can be harmful to its health.

If choosing a ceramic bowl, you must be absolutely sure that it was not fired with a lead-based glaze. Also, unless you enjoy cleaning your floors three times a day, make sure that your dog's dishes are not tippable.

The Collar and Leash

A collar and a leash are also mandatory equipment. Collars and leashes come in a variety of sizes and are made of several different materials, including leather, nylon, and metal chain. The Cocker owner need not worry about the dog's strength and, therefore, needs only a well-made leather or nylon collar and leash. Leather and nylon equipment, however, should be checked from time to time because they tend to deteriorate with age. If you are getting a puppy, you may also find it necessary to buy collars of different sizes to accommodate the dog's growing body. You should consider buying a special collar equipped with a slip ring, which will help during training sessions.

Note: It is important to assure that the training collar fits and the slip ring functions properly. If the slip ring does not properly release, it can actually choke the dog.

TIP

Reflective Tape

I recommend using reflective tape or tags on both the collar and the walking leashes. These will render both you and your dog more visible to car drivers and thereby make your nighttime walks much safer. You should attach to your dog's collar an identity tag that gives your name, address, and telephone number. This inexpensive tag could prove invaluable should your beloved pet ever become lost.

You may also wish to have several leashes on hand. For regular walks or training, you need a leash that is only several feet long. For outdoor fun, a long leash equipped with an automatic reel permits more freedom. If you have a puppy, you should check his leash regularly for chew marks; chewing can quickly weaken a nylon or leather leash. Also, be sure that your puppy never chews on the leash's metal clips, which can damage its teeth.

The Muzzle

Only very rarely will a Cocker Spaniel require a muzzle. However, a dog in severe pain may act unpredictably and may snap at his owner, so it is best to be prepared. When buying a muzzle, select one that can be adjusted to fit both young and adult Cockers.

Other Equipment

Additional equipment and accessories that you should have on hand are flea spray and tweezers to combat external parasites, and grooming supplies. All of these items are listed in detail in HOW-TO: Grooming (pages 38–39).

To avoid added stress to what is already likely to be a hectic day, you should buy all your Cocker's equipment before you bring your new pet home. Then pick out a single place to store the items so that they will be easily accessible when the need for any of them arises.

Toys

The Importance of Toys

As a new dog owner, you should never underestimate the importance of toys for your pet. Toys play a vital role in keeping your dog both physically and mentally fit. They can give your Cocker added exercise, and many have the ability to keep your pet busy and entertained for long periods of time—an added benefit on occasions when you cannot closely supervise your

Cocker. For instance, when you are cooking dinner, you can keep your dog out of mischief simply by giving him a favorite toy to play with.

While it may seem strange, toys also have some psychological benefits for your Cocker. In the wild, doglike creatures are organized in a social structure where the dominant animals become pack leaders while smaller, weaker animals are followers. During training sessions you will actually be enforcing your superiority as master over your pet. Eventually your Cocker will come to understand that all of the members of your family are above him in the social structure of your household. In this situation, toys can serve as objects for your dog to dominate, enabling him to work out the frustration that he may feel from always having to be submissive to the humans in your household.

Toys serve an additional purpose for a Cocker puppy in that they help sharpen his hunting and survival skills. Even though your Cocker may not have received any formal training as a hunting dog, you will notice that the breed has inherited instinctive behavior patterns common to most gundogs. Your puppy will naturally stalk, attempt to flush, and finally capture its toys just as an older bird dog may do with living prey.

If you are still unconvinced of the importance of toys, here is one last reason to get them: a dog toy is cheaper than new furniture. Teething puppies spend a lot of time chewing in an attempt to strengthen their teeth and jaw muscles. Nylon and rawhide bones make excellent chew toys, and will satisfy their urge and in the process, spare the Chippendale. Both are good teeth-cleaners and pacifiers, and are safe. Some experts say that rawhide chew sticks are dangerous and should be avoided; however, I have used them for decades and have never had a problem.

Safety Notes

Because a puppy's teeth are sharp, you will have to keep a watchful eye on his toys.

Rawhide bones must be replaced before they become small enough to swallow whole. Avoid soft toys that can be shredded and swallowed by an active puppy. Swallowing large or foreign objects can cause choking or a blockage in the puppy's digestive system.

Be sure that all of your Cocker's "chew" toys are designed for dogs and are made of non-toxic materials. Remember that many forms of plastic are toxic, and soft woods tend to splinter. To be safe, avoid all painted or varnished toys, as these may contain chemicals that can be harmful to your pet. Finally, monitor your dog's toys and discard any that start to break into pieces or fray.

Homemade Toys

Other types of toys can be created from simple household objects. Playing "hide-and-seek" using a cardboard box or paper shopping bag can keep your puppy busy for hours. Tennis balls also make good toys, because they are durable enough to stand up to a puppy's teeth, yet too big to be swallowed whole. Obviously, you should avoid letting your puppy have small or breakable objects. Also, it is inadvisable to give your puppy personal items that have your scent on them, such as old slippers or sneakers. While the Cocker Spaniel is an intelligent dog, chances are that your pet will not be able to tell the difference between your old and new footwear.

CARING FOR A COCKER SPANIEL

It is inevitable that your first days home with your new puppy will be rather hectic. To reduce the worry, confusion, and stress to both you and your pet, certain precautions should be taken.

Preparing for a Puppy

1. If at all possible, visit your puppy several times before you bring her home to help her become familiar with your presence. Recognizing a friendly face will help reduce the stress the puppy will feel when she finds herself in a totally new environment away from her mother and siblings.

2. Lay in the supplies and prepare the housing for your pet. Find out from the breeder what kind of food the puppy has been fed and buy a supply ahead of time. Using the same kind of food will reduce the chances of dietary upsets. At the same time you should also purchase all the equipment and accessories mentioned in the preceding chapter and store them in a convenient place. Then lay out your puppy's eating and sleeping areas.

3. The next step in preparing for the new arrival is to "puppy-proof" your home.

4. Make sure that your friends and family understand the basic rules of handling a Cocker puppy.

5. Finally, if at all possible, bring the puppy home on a weekend or at another time when you have a few days off. This way you can stay close to the little newcomer, supervise her for a few days in a row, and start forming a strong bond with each other.

"Puppy-proofing" Your Home

An essential step in preparing for your new friend is to make sure you bring her into a "puppy-friendly" environment. When "puppy-proofing" your home, keep in mind that a young dog is an extremely inquisitive creature and will investigate every square inch of your house or apartment, using her nose to sniff, paws to touch, and teeth to chew just about everything she encounters. Therefore, you will have to remove all potential hazards from your puppy's reach—and you will be amazed at just how small a nook or how high a cranny your puppy can get into.

The Rules of Puppy Safety

Before bringing your new puppy home, review these seven rules with your family and friends. In addition to preventing injury, these rules will help your puppy to feel comfortable and safe in her new home, and increase her confidence in you and your family.

1 Avoid unnecessary excitement. New owners have a tendency to invite everyone they know over to see the new member of their family, and young visitors will usually run around screaming with excitement. Let the puppy adjust to her new surroundings in peace before subjecting her to numerous strangers.

2 Prohibit rough play. Puppies are very fragile creatures and should be handled with care until they grow larger and are more mature. Avoid overhandling and make sure the children do not prod or poke the puppy, play with her ears, or subject her to any other rough handling.

3 Be sure everyone in your household knows the proper way to lift and carry your puppy. The proper technique is described in detail later in this chapter. If any visitors want to pick up the puppy, instruct them how to do so.

4 Avoid picking up the puppy too much. Allow her to do her own walking as much as possible. This will allow her to get her exercise as well as improve her motor skills and physical abilities.

5 Do not give bones or other hard objects to a young puppy. Until a puppy reaches about six months of age, she has only her milk teeth and cannot chew hard objects.

6 Do not subject your puppy to unnecessary heights. Avoid placing her on tables, counters, or beds, because a fall could be disastrous. When it is necessary to place the puppy on an elevated surface, such as when you are examining or grooming her, someone must be present the entire time to assure the puppy's safety.

7 Try never to leave the puppy unsupervised during the first few weeks.

Remove Puppy Hazards

Remove all sharp objects such as staples and nails from your home. Be sure that all electrical cords and wires are out of your puppy's reach; the shock received from chewing on a live electric wire can severely injure and even kill a dog. You should also place all poisons such as paints, disinfectants, insecticides, cleaners, and antifreeze in a location that is completely secure from infiltration by a determined puppy.

Once you have puppy-proofed your house, check your yard and garage and again remove all potentially harmful materials. For your puppy's safety, be thorough when checking for hazardous situations, and follow this adage: "When in doubt (of an object's safety), move it out (of your puppy's reach)."

The First Days Home

The Trip Home

The big day has finally arrived—you are to pick up your puppy and bring her to her new home. When you go to the breeder or pet dealer be sure to bring your Cocker's collar, leash, and traveling cage with you. It is extremely unwise to let your puppy loose in your car on the journey home, no matter how short the distance. If you will have to travel for several hours, bring along a little food and water, and plan on making a stop or two to allow your puppy to eat, drink, and relieve herself.

If you have to travel for a considerable distance, there is always the chance that your puppy will become carsick. As a precaution, bring extra blankets to line your puppy's traveling cage in case of accidents. You will also need a short-bristled brush and some towels to clean the dog's coat. Do not wash the dog with water, because it can lead to a chill if she is exposed to drafts.

Upon Arrival

Once you have reached home, put your puppy on the leash, let her walk around outside for a while, and take her to the site you have chosen for her elimination area. Do not rush the puppy inside; give her plenty of time to relieve herself. In this way there will be one less thing for you to worry about when the puppy is taken indoors.

The Apprehensive Puppy

Make your puppy's first days in your house as stress-free as possible. Keep visitors to a minimum, and allow your little friend time to get used to her new family before you intro-

duce her to neighbors and friends. A calm, quiet atmosphere will help to reassure your puppy that she will be safe and loved in her new home.

Let your pet spend her first few hours exploring your house or apartment. Take every opportunity to speak soft words and pet her reassuringly. Show the puppy where her food and water dishes are, and if she wants to eat or drink, let her do so in peace. To reduce the effects of stress on your puppy's digestive system, feed her the same food, on the same time schedule, that the breeder used. When the puppy tires, pick her up and place her in her cage or sleeping box to rest. After a few days, the puppy will learn to seek out her sleeping area on her own.

The First Nights

During her first day in your home, you can expect your puppy to take several short naps. She is unlikely, however, to sleep throughout

Sleeping

It is extremely important that a puppy learns to sleep alone in her own bed. If the puppy whines, pick her up and quickly bring her to a previously chosen outdoor elimination spot and place her on the ground. When the pup has urinated or defecated, pick her up, return her to the crate, and then you should return to your own bed. If the puppy does not go after a sufficient amount of time has passed, then return her to the cage and go to your bed. If the whining continues, try sitting next to your puppy's bed, calming with soothing words or petting her, but do not pick her up and comfort her. The puppy needs to learn how to behave when she is alone, and it is best to start this lesson as soon as possible. So, as soon as she calms down, go back to your own bed.

To reduce the stress of being separated from her mother and siblings, spend some time preparing for the long night to come.

the night. Usually the puppy will wake up and, finding herself in a dark and strange place, will begin to whine and whimper for her mother and siblings.

When your puppy looks tired, put her in her bed with a few toys. Draw the curtains and turn out the lights to make the room as dark as possible. Then leave the room, making sure that the puppy cannot get out and cannot see or hear you. Most likely, your puppy will begin to cry. If this happens, wait at least five minutes before returning. Should the puppy settle

down, let at least ten minutes pass before reentering the room. Repeating this procedure several times during the day should help to lessen the feelings of isolation and alienation that your puppy will experience at night.

Home Alone

Don't leave your puppy alone for long periods of time for the first few days. In addition to the emotional stress, an unsupervised puppy can get into a lot of trouble. If you must leave, have a relative, neighbor, or close friend "puppy sit," preferably in your home. Taking your puppy to another strange place will only multiply its anxiety.

After a few weeks, when your Cocker has begun to feel completely comfortable in your home, and has gained your trust and confidence, you can begin to leave her alone for longer and longer periods. Regardless of how confident you are, however, I advise you to limit your puppy's access to the portion of your home that contains her feeding and sleeping areas. Also, be sure to inspect these rooms again to assure that no potential hazards are within your puppy's reach.

Lifting and Carrying

The Proper Technique

To prevent injuries, be sure that everyone in your family, as well as visitors, learns how to lift and carry your puppy. The proper technique requires that one hand be under the puppy's chest, while the other hand is placed behind the dog to support her rear end and hind legs. Never pick a puppy up by the scruff of the

neck or with one hand under her abdomen. Both of these methods can hurt the dog.

There are few times when it is necessary to carry an adult Cocker. You should avoid pampering your dog by carrying her up a flight of stairs or outside to her run. Let your Cocker get as much exercise as she can, and lift and carry her only when absolutely necessary. If you find that you must lift your adult Cocker, place one hand under the chest and the other supporting the hindquarters.

The Injured Dog

Should your dog become severely injured and need to be taken to the veterinarian, you will be well advised to put on the dog's muzzle before moving the animal. A dog that is in severe pain

may act unpredictably, and may snap at or bite anyone who tries to help her. Once the threat of biting has been eliminated, you can lift the dog by placing one arm between both the front and

The proper way to hold your puppy.

the rear pair of legs and resting the dog's head in the crook of your arm, thereby keeping her from falling forward. You can also move an injured dog by placing her on her side on a blanket, which can serve as a stretcher.

On the Road Again

Many people consider their dogs to be members of their family; as such, they are always taken on family trips and vacations. If you are such a person, and wish to take your Cocker wherever you go, a little planning is all it takes to make everything go smoothly.

Traveling with Your Dog

The key to traveling with your Cocker is planning, and finding the specific rules you will need to adhere to. Not all airlines, cruise ships, and trains accept dogs, and many have significant restrictions. For example, some airlines will transport dogs only when the temperatures are between 35°F and 85°F (1.7°C to 29.5°C) on both ends of the flight, and some will not let dogs travel in the passenger cabin, only the cargo hold, so be sure to read the rules on the carrier's web site. In the United States, federal law requires that dogs traveling by air must be certified by a veterinarian within 10 days of the trip to be healthy, vaccinated, and free from contagious diseases. You may also have to deal with security. When you check in your baggage you will also need to check in your dog. To do this you will need to remove the dog from her travel crate, which is put onto the conveyor and goes through the X-ray check. The dog will go with you through the metal detector, so be sure you remove any metal ID tags.

If you are going to travel abroad, obtain a copy of the rules pertaining to pets from the consulate of the country you will visit. Some countries have the same requirements as you would find for a domestic trip. Others are stricter, and may require that your dog remain in quarantine while they determine its health status. The key to being able to relax more while on vacation is to plan your dog-friendly travel schedule and accommodations as thoroughly as possible.

When traveling by car, it is best to keep your dog in her cage. When driving, open the window enough to give your dog fresh air, but be careful not to expose her to drafts, which can cause eye, ear, and respiratory problems. Make a rest stop at least every two hours, and walk your dog on a leash, giving her ample time to relieve herself. Allow your dog to drink regularly. Keep her water in a bottle on the floor of the car, where it will remain cool. If your dog tends to get carsick, you should obtain tablets for motion sickness from your veterinarian. Place an inexpensive thermometer in the cage or crate. Check it regularly to be sure that your dog is not being exposed to temperatures that are either too cool or too warm. You can help regulate the temperature the dog is exposed to by changing the position of the travel crate in the car, or adjusting the car's heater or air conditioner.

When packing for your Cocker, be sure to include her grooming equipment, food and water dishes, leash, muzzle, cage, blanket, and, if possible, enough food to last the entire trip. Travel will probably cause additional stress to your dog's digestive system. By feeding your pet the type of food she is accustomed to, you can help to minimize digestive upsets.

Leaving Your Dog at Home

If you choose not to take your dog when you travel, I recommend having a friend or relative look after her. Optimally, the "dogsitter" will come to your house whenever necessary. In this way, your dog can stay in a familiar environment. If the person cannot come to your home, then perhaps he or she would consider keeping your Cocker in his or her own house while you are away.

If you cannot find a trustworthy person to take care of your Cocker, you will have to resort to a boarding kennel. Before you decide, however, inspect the kennel to make sure that it is clean and well managed, and that the proprietor can and will meet your Cocker's special needs.

You should be aware that Cocker Spaniels can be very temperamental and do not always take well to being away from their masters for long periods of time.

Regular Brushing

Start by using the slicker brush to thoroughly brush the dog's back and sides, avoiding all the areas of the body with longer hair. Use the pin brush for the feathered hair on the legs, abdomen, chest, and ears. Be sure to remove all stubborn tangles and matted areas while brushing. Once brushing is complete, use a comb to remove all loose hairs. Whenever you are brushing your Cocker you should look for signs of flea infestation (see "Fleas" in the "Ailments and Illnesses" section). If you notice any other skin condition, seek the advice of your veterinarian.

Ear and Eye Care

During these regular sessions, pay particular attention to your Cocker's ears. Like most long-eared breeds, Cockers are prone to ear trouble. To avoid serious infections, trim all excess hair from the ear canals. A pair of tweezers is handy to remove any loose hairs that have gotten into the ear. Carefully remove any wax buildup using a commercial ear-cleaning solution. To clean the ear, hold it open with one hand and gently clean the inside of the flap with a cotton ball dipped in cleaning solution. Use a fresh cotton ball for each ear. You can clean the outermost portions of the ear canal using a cotton swab that has been dipped in the solution.

Inspect your Cocker's eyes regularly as well, to be sure they are clear and free of any discharge. You can clean around your dog's eyes with a moistened cotton ball to remove any dirt. Again, use a fresh cotton ball for each eye. If you notice any damage or inflammation, contact your veterinarian for advice.

Caution: Before cleaning your dog's eyes and ears for the first time, I recommend that you consult with your veterinarian for the proper way to clean and handle them. An inexperienced owner can cause serious harm to a dog while probing around.

Nail and Paw Care

When trimming the coat, check the bottoms of the dog's paws and trim the hair between the toes as short as possible. This will improve the dog's traction and reduce the chance of infection in wet weather. If your Cocker is active, you may not need to trim her nails very often. However, the nails of the average house dog can grow back quite rapidly and will require frequent trimming. Before you trim your dog's nails learn how to use a pair of clippers. Improper use can cause your dog a great deal of pain. An experienced dog groomer or veterinarian can show you how to use them.

The center of the dog's nail is called the "quick" and contains the blood vessels and nerve endings. You can see them when you examine the dog's nails. If you cut the quick, you will cause the dog much

Equipment

Every Cocker owner should own the following: a comb, a slicker brush, a pin brush, scissors, nail clippers, tweezers, ear cleaning solution, and cotton swabs. Many people also find it advantageous to have electric trimmers and a wide variety of combs, brushes, and scissors. While absolutely necessary for professional groomers and handlers, the average dog owner would have trouble justifying the cost. Because the Cocker is a relatively small dog, and she is easier to groom when she is at "table level," you may also want to consider the purchase of a grooming table. These tables usually come equipped with a restraining harness that will be very helpful should you find yourself with an unwilling pet.

pain. In addition, the quick grows out as the nail lengthens. If you wait too long between pedicures, you may have to cut the quick in order to get the nail back to a comfortable length. Always cut the nail as close to the quick as possible, and be sure to hold your pet's paw firmly but gently. If you cut the nail too short it will bleed, so be sure to have styptic powder on hand.

Tooth Care

Tooth care begins with feeding your Cocker plenty of hard foods, such as dog biscuits and rawhide bones, to prevent the buildup of tartar. Excessive tartar can lead to the deterioration of the gums and tooth loss. You should also brush your dog's teeth once a week with a commercial toothpaste that is formulated specifically for dogs. Before brushing, check the dog's teeth and gums for signs of infection and tartar buildup. Excessive tartar can be scraped off by your veterinarian.

Bathing

In general, bathing should be thought of as a last resort. While shampooing your Cocker helps to eliminate dirt and "doggie odors," it can remove much of the natural oils that weatherproof the coat. Excessive bathing will also tend to dry out your Cocker's skin and promote excessive shedding. Whenever possible try to clean your dog with a wet, slightly soapy cloth.

When bathing does become necessary, use a high-quality shampoo formulated specifically for dogs, and be sure to rinse out all of the shampoo, because it may irritate the dog's skin. Dry your Cocker by rubbing her briskly with a towel. If you wish to accelerate the process, use a blow dryer. Once most of the water has been removed, brush and comb out the coat. Keep your dog indoors and away from drafts while she is drying.

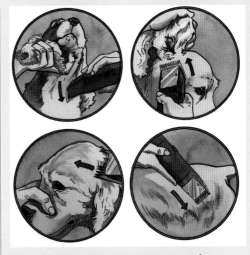

When trimming it is important to move the clippers in the proper direction.

Note: It is especially important to avoid giving a puppy a bath until she is at least six months old or until she has had her permanent vaccinations. Puppies are particularly susceptible to drafts and can become sick after being soaked to the skin. If a bath is absolutely necessary, be sure to dry the puppy thoroughly and keep her in a warm, draft-free area for several hours afterward.

Once a week, use a toothbrush topped with baking soda or a specially formulated dog toothpaste to prevent the formation of tartar.

WHAT DO I FEED MY DOG?

The nutritional requirements of dogs have probably not changed very much from the time they were first domesticated. Our understanding of those needs, however, has increased greatly in recent years.

The National Research Council (NRC), a division of the National Academy of Science of the United States, has interpreted vast quantities of data and published a study entitled "The Nutritional Requirements of Dogs." This study establishes the minimum amount of every nutrient (protein, fat, carbohydrates, vitamins, minerals, and trace elements) needed to maintain the health of the average middle-age and older adult dog, as well as growing puppies.

The NRC study is used by practically all companies that manufacture commercial dog food in the United States, to help them formulate their products. In fact, for a dog food to be certified as "complete and balanced" in the United States, it must meet or exceed all of the nutritional requirements established by the NRC, and must pass actual feeding tests as established by the Association of American Feed Control Officials (AAFCO).

While their ancestors, wolves, are scientifically classified as carnivores, modern domestic dogs have evolved to a point where they can effectively utilize a wide variety of foodstuffs

to meet their nutritional needs, and are therefore considered omnivores. This allows modern commercial dog food manufacturers to use a wide variety of ingredients to achieve the mandated nutritional profiles, but makes it very hard to determine which dog food is best for your Cocker. To help decide, seek the advice of your breeder and veterinarian. Breeders will know what food works best on their Cockers, while veterinarians have a working knowledge of dog foods based on the experiences of other clients. A veterinarian will also be able to recommend a special diet should your Cocker's health dictate the need for one.

As you can probably guess, I strongly urge all dog owners to use a high-quality commercial dog food, rather than preparing their pet's food from scratch. When preparing meals at home, it becomes all too easy to give your pet either too much or too little of an essential nutrient. This process is significantly more expensive and much more time-consuming (time you can instead be playing and exercising with your beloved pet). If, however, you feel

that you want to prepare your dog's food fresh, as an act of love, then I strongly advise you to read as many books as you can on animal nutrition, and seek the advice of your veterinarian.

What Is High Quality?

Like human food recipes, the ingredients used to make commercial dog foods have a varying degree of nutritional value. While most complete diets are supplemented with a sufficient quantity of vitamins and minerals, the ingredients used in a high-quality dog food should be easily digestible and free of chemical additives, which over the long term can have harmful effects on your pet.

When looking for a high-quality diet, check the label to make sure the pet food was tested using AAFCO procedures and is complete and balanced. This statement can be found at the end of the nutritional information panel. Check the ingredients listing. By law, the label must contain a list of ingredients, with the most abundant ingredient (by percent weight) listed first, and continue in a descending order. The primary ingredients listed in a high-quality dog food should be easily recognizable, such as chicken, beef, lamb, brown rice, carrots, and peas. Ingredients such as cornmeal, wheat, soy, and white rice are carbohydrate fillers that are not easy to digest and provide little nutritional value. Be extra cautious with wheat and soy-based products as they are both allergens. Look for foods that use meat meals, rather than animal "by-products." Meat meal is actually meat with the water removed, where "by-products" contain the indigestible parts of animals including feet, feathers, hooves, and hair. Finally, avoid foods that contain chemical antioxidants such as BHA and BHT. High-quality dog foods will instead use vitamin C or vitamin E to prevent fats from oxidizing.

Feeding Table Scraps

Many people feel that they are obliged as loving pet owners to feed their precious pooches their leftovers. Be warned that this practice has great potential for teaching your Cocker really bad habits, such as begging. In addition, it can also lead the dog to refuse his regular food, which, in turn, can cause nutritional problems. It can also lead to obesity, which can cause many other problems later on.

How Many Meals Do I Feed My Dog?

Relative to their body weight, dogs eat larger quantities of food than humans, so they do not need to be fed as frequently. Adults can be fed one or two times a day, while puppies need to be fed more often. A puppy between four weeks and three months old needs to be fed at least four times a day, while puppies between three and five months old can be fed three times a day. Because dogs react well to routines, you should create a schedule that you can commit to and stick with. A good time to feed your dog is during the family meals, so he is occupied while the rest of the family is at the dinner table.

dog has an adequate supply of water at all times. A Cocker's water intake will depend on several factors, including air temperature, the type of food he eats, the amount of exercise he gets, and his temperament. Be sure to avoid giving your dog very cold water, especially after strenuous exercise or if he is showing signs of heatstroke. Cooling the dog's body down too fast can be counterproductive and lead to other severe illnesses.

The Importance of Water

Of all the nutrients in a dog's diet, there is none more important than water. Water is vital to every living cell and comprises nearly 60 percent of your dog's body weight. Unlike some animals, dogs cannot store much water and must constantly replenish whatever they lose. This means that you must make sure your

Does My Cocker Need Nutritional Supplements?

This is a very controversial topic at the moment. While there is plenty of information available, it can become difficult to separate the information that comes from the manufacturers of these various nutritional supplements from that of independent researchers.

Naturally, the manufacturers of these items are interested in selling their products, but, as in humans, getting too much of some nutrients (such as vitamin D) can be toxic, and have dangerous side effects. The amount of nutrients your dog needs will depend on several factors, including diet, age, activity level, medical conditions, and environmental stresses, so not all dogs need nutritional supplements, while others may have very specific needs.

Before giving your dog any supplement, particularly a vitamin or mineral supplement, you should consult with your veterinarian. He or she will review with you the critical factors affecting your dog's nutritional requirements before giving you advice.

Special Considerations in Feeding Your Cocker

While the NRC provides the minimum nutritional requirements for puppies, adult, and older dogs, several other factors affect the type and quantity of food an individual dog needs. Growing puppies require about twice the amount of calories per pound of body weight as a middle-aged adult, while older dogs require about 20 percent less than an average adult. Puppies, therefore, need special diets that are higher in proteins and fats to support their growth and metabolic needs. Because older dogs have a slower metabolism, they can become overweight if the diet is not changed. Exercise, work performed, and environment will also influence the quantity of food your Cocker needs. Cockers that get a lot of exercise, are used for hunting, or participate in numerous field and obedience trials will usually require a diet that is higher in calories. The same is true for dogs that spend a lot of time outdoors in the cold weather.

The best indicators that a dog is getting the proper amount of nutrition are his body weight and coat condition. Your dog is at an ideal weight if you can feel his ribs, and can easily discern the waist from the ribs, when looking from above. You should also be able to feel the abdomen tucked up. If you have an underweight Cocker, you will easily see his ribs, vertebrae, and pelvic bones, and you will not

feel any fat on the bones. Severely malnourished dogs lose muscle mass, and puppies will have stunted growth. When a Cocker is overweight, you cannot feel the ribs, and you may see fat deposits over his back. In addition, the waist will not be discernable from the ribs when viewed from above, and the abdomen will drop. A dry coat and flaky skin may signify a fat, fatty acid, or vitamin deficiency. This condition is often accompanied by scratching and is many times misdiagnosed by pet owners as external parasites or other skin ailments. The proper diet should produce a soft and shiny coat that is rich in color.

A final note on feeding a dog: You should know that dogs do not require a wide variety of foods, and will not tire from eating the same thing every day. If you feed your Cocker a high-quality, well-balanced diet, he can thrive on that food for most of his life. If your dog is not eating properly it may be an indicator of a physical or emotional problem. If your Cocker falls off of his diet for a day or two, there may not be any reason to worry and the dog's appetite may return on its own. But if your dog refuses to eat for more than two days, then it may be a sign of a serious problem and the dog should be taken to the veterinarian for an examination.

AILMENTS AND ILLNESSES

Dogs, like humans, are subject to a wide variety of illnesses. While the Cocker Spaniel is no exception, you will be glad to know that there are several things you can do to prevent many of the ailments described in this chapter.

In General

Proper nutrition, good hygiene, and an adequate exercise program are essential in keeping your Cocker healthy. By providing these requisites, combined with scheduled visits to the veterinarian for booster shots and routine examinations, you can help your Cocker to live a long and healthy life. You must never underestimate the importance of keeping scheduled appointments with your veterinarian. Early detection is the key in preventing many problems from getting out of hand, and it sometimes takes a trained medical eye to detect early symptoms.

Choosing a Veterinarian

It is safe to say that the worst time to look for a veterinarian is when you really need one, so make sure you have chosen the right veterinarian for you before you bring your new Cocker home. When looking for a veterinarian,

keep in mind that you are looking for more than a medical expert. You're looking for someone to meet the needs of both you and your pet; someone with "people" as well as "animal" skills.

Like your doctor, veterinarians often work with a staff of professionals (technicians, administrators, and aides), so you will likely want to evaluate the competence and caring of the entire team. Location, fees, facility cleanliness, and suitability are also very important factors that you will need to evaluate. Weigh all of the issues that are important to you, but remember you will probably be happier if you drive a few extra miles or pay a few extra dollars to get the care you want for your Cocker.

The best way to find a good veterinarian is to ask people who have the same approach to pet care as you. Look for recommendations from friends, animal shelters, dog trainers, groomers, or pet sitters. Once you've narrowed your search, schedule a visit to meet the staff, tour the facility, and learn about the veterinary philosophy on treatment and the hospital's policies.

Once you feel you have completed your research it is time to make your choice. Only you can determine what factors are the most important, but under no circumstances should this decision ever be made by cost alone.

What Are Symptoms?

Simply put, symptoms are indicators of diseases or disorders; and because dogs cannot talk, symptoms provide the only means by which you can infer that your pet is not feeling well. Although understanding the symptoms or combinations of symptoms associated with certain ailments may help you narrow down the possibilities, the trained eye of a veterinarian is usually required to determine the exact cause.

Symptoms to Watch For

There are several symptoms of which every dog owner should be aware. If you notice any one, or a combination of them, you should call your veterinarian. Be alert for

✔ physical exhaustion
✔ loss of appetite or thirst
✔ excessive appetite or thirst
✔ unusual sneezing or wheezing
✔ excessive coughing
✔ runny nose
✔ discharge from the eyes or ears
✔ poor coat condition
✔ foul breath
✔ blood in the stool
✔ slight paralysis
✔ limping, trembling, or shaking
✔ swelling or lumps on the body
✔ sudden weight loss
✔ cloudy or orange-colored urine
✔ inability to urinate

✔ uncontrolled urination
✔ moaning or whimpering
✔ unusual slobbering or salivation
✔ vomiting
✔ diarrhea

The last two, vomiting and diarrhea, are probably the most common of all canine symptoms. However, they do not always indicate the presence of a serious ailment.

For instance, young dogs sometimes attack their food with such reckless abandon that their natural defensive mechanisms send the food back up again. It is also common to see a dog eat grass and subsequently vomit in a voluntary attempt to purge the digestive tract. While this behavior is completely natural, it may be an indicator that a larger problem exists.

Persistent vomiting, however, can indicate a very serious ailment, and should be reported to your veterinarian immediately. It can be caused by several digestive disorders and diseases, and is often accompanied by irregular bowel movements, including diarrhea.

Likewise, the occasional soft stool is usually nothing to worry about. During the warmer summer months, dogs tend to drink more water, and as a result, their stools may become loose, or they may even get diarrhea. Short-term acute diarrhea can also be caused by minor stomach upsets. Acute diarrhea starts suddenly and lasts for a few days to a week or two. Most cases of acute diarrhea can be handled at home, by changing your dog's diet.

Chronic diarrhea (continuous or frequent watery bowel movements, where your dog is acting sick during the worst bouts), on the other hand, can indicate a serious problem. Long-standing diarrhea can become a severely debilitating disorder. It can cause your dog's body to lose valuable nutrients, become depleted of immune system functions, and lose its ability to properly detoxify. This in turn can lead to the development of secondary disorders that will make the problem even harder to treat. Whenever you see the signs of chronic diarrhea, it needs to be brought to the immediate attention of your veterinarian.

Immunization: Pros and Cons

Before the discovery of vaccines, several infectious diseases ran rampant through the canine population, leading to a large number of deaths. Most of these diseases are caused by bacteria or viruses that dogs can contract from a wide variety of sources. Advances in modern medical science led to the development of vaccines that can protect dogs against most major infectious diseases. While all vaccines are extremely effective, however, not all are needed by every dog, and not all offer permanent protection. For years the standard practice was to give booster shots for those with limited protection. And in some cases, the frequency in which they are required to be given is determined by local law. This "better safe than sorry" practice, however, is presently the topic of heavy debate.

For decades, homeopaths have been arguing against frequent vaccination, claiming that vaccines are not as benign as first believed, and dogs that are vaccinated excessively or needlessly are subject to more diseases and disorders than dogs that are not. In addition, many veterinary schools have begun researching the long-term effects of vaccines, in order to determine if the effect they have on the long-range health of the dog outweighs the benefits gained from the presently recommended vaccination protocol.

Another approach being used to determine the need to revaccinate is called *titer (titre) testing*. This test is used to determine the levels of specific disease-fighting antibodies the dog has in his bloodstream. If the titer test reveals sufficient levels of a specific disease-fighting antibody, then it is a good indicator that the dog has immunity against the disease and revaccination may not be needed. Unfortunately, a low or absent titer does not always indicate that the dog does not have immunity. A dog's immune system has a "memory" and will not expend energy developing unnecessary antibodies if it has the ability to produce more within a day or two of exposure to an infec-

tious organism. So while titer testing will tell if a dog has a level of antibody to give him a reasonable chance to fight a disease, it can give false negatives that could lead to unnecessary booster vaccinations.

So where does this leave the average dog owner? My recommendation is to treat vaccine administration as a medical procedure, and as such, the benefits as well as risks need to be considered when making the decision to use them. Talk to your veterinarian about your concerns. In return, listen to the reasoning they used in determining the frequency recommended for vaccination (which comes from practical experience). If you believe that your veterinarian has your pet's best interest in mind, then the choice is usually very easy. Keep in mind, however, that sometimes, the frequency of vaccination is required by law.

Infectious Diseases and Vaccines

In the United States, vaccines are now divided into two classes. "Core" vaccines are those that should be given to every dog, and "noncore" vaccines are recommended only for certain dogs, depending on their species and environment. The choice to use noncore vaccines depends on a number of variables, including age, breed, the health status of the dog, the potential of exposure, the type of vaccine, and how common the disease is to the geographical area where the dog lives. So, dogs that are not boarded probably do not need all the vaccinations against "kennel cough," and the Lyme disease vaccine should be administered only if you live in an area where it is prevalent. It is important to note, that some core and noncore vaccines are given by veterinarians in what are called "combination vaccines," which means

that a single injection will deliver the vaccines for as many as five different contagious diseases. Determining what "combination" and noncore vaccines, as well as the type and frequency of booster immunizations, your dog receives is a decision that you will have to make with the advice of your veterinarian.

The four core vaccines immunize your Cocker against canine distemper, canine hepatitis, parvovirus, and rabies. Recently, however, a report from the American Veterinary Medical Association (AVMA) recommends adding canine adenovirus-2 (presently classified as noncore) to the core vaccines. Noncore vaccines also exist for bordetellosis, parainfluenza, leptospirosis, coronavirus, and Lyme disease. Chances are that your breeder will have your puppy up to date on its immunizations when you get him. As it takes three to four weeks for the first sets of immunizations to become completely effective, it would be wise to keep your new puppy away from all nonimmunized animals until the vaccines can take full effect.

Internal Parasites

Worms are by far the most common internal parasite found in dogs. There are four major types of worms that live in the digestive tract (roundworms, hookworms, whipworms, and tapeworms) of the infected animal and one major type that attacks the heart muscle (heartworms). The eggs of the digestive tract worms, and sometimes adult worms themselves, can be found in the dog's stool. The eggs are microscopic, so if you suspect your dog has worms, you will have to take a stool sample to the veterinarian so the proper medication can be given.

Roundworms

These parasites are commonly seen in young dogs. They are white, cylindrical in shape, and can grow up to 4 inches (10 cm) long. During their life cycle, roundworm larvae migrate through various organs in the dog's body and will finish their migration in the intestinal tract, where they become adults and lay their eggs, which are passed out with the stool. The larvae will also migrate to the womb of pregnant females where they can infest the unborn puppies. If the eggs are ingested by another animal, they will grow into adults in their new host and thus continue the cycle. While roundworms are rarely harmful to an adult dog, they can be fatal to a puppy.

Symptoms of roundworms include diarrhea, cramps, irregular appetite, weakness, poor coat condition, bloated belly, and in severe cases, paralysis. They can be treated with an oral de-worming medication. All fecal matter expelled during the treatment phase needs to be picked up and disposed of to keep the dog from ingesting more eggs. There are heartworm medications on the market that are also effective in controlling roundworms (as well as hookworms, whipworms, and tapeworms).

Roundworms pose a public health hazard as the larvae can penetrate human skin and affect various organs in the body. So, avoid being barefoot before and during treatment, and wash thoroughly when cleaning up after your Cocker.

Hookworms

These are also most commonly seen in younger dogs, live in the intestines, and pass their eggs out in the host's stool. They are light in color and resemble long strings of spaghetti. Dogs become infected by eating the eggs, pen-etration of the footpads or skin by the larvae, transmission through nursing mother's milk, or passed from a mother to her unborn puppies. Hookworm infestations can cause fatal anemia in young, weak, or malnourished dogs.

Symptoms include weight loss, diarrhea, and bloody stools, and sometimes adult worms are seen in the feces. Treatment also includes treating anemia if it accompanies the infesta-tion. As hookworms are also public health threats, follow the same precautions regarding cleaning up, personal sanitization, and apparel, as listed for roundworms.

Whipworms

These worms are normally seen in dogs that are three months of age or older, as the eggs will not be seen in the stool until three months after the infection. The adult worms live in the large intestine, and the eggs are passed through the stool. Diagnosis can sometimes be difficult because, unlike all of the other diges-tive tract worms, whipworms are not prolific egg layers. Infection occurs when a dog eats contaminated fecal matter.

Symptoms of whipworm infestations include loss of weight, and diarrhea that is sometimes tinted with blood. These worms are usually not seen in the stool. Treatment consists of using an oral de-wormer with follow-up doses.

Tapeworms

Adults live in the intestines of dogs and are transmitted to the victim by eating fleas that have in turn ingested tapeworm eggs. Some forms of tapeworms can also be carried by small mammals and if ingested can grow in the new host. The head of the worm has a series of hooks that it uses to attach itself tenaciously to a dog's small intestine. The body of a tapeworm grows in a long, segmented chain with the tail section containing many eggs. On occasion the worm will release the egg-containing section that is then passed out in the stool. These sections look like grains of rice and often stick to the hairs around a dog's anus.

The symptoms of tapeworm infestations take a long time to develop and include poor coat condition, irritability, diarrhea, and lethargy. Treatment is with an oral de-worming medication or an injection. Control of infestations can be achieved by preventing exposure of the dog to fleas. While people can become infected from certain species of tapeworms that can be found in dogs, these instances are very rare.

Heartworms

While once found only found along the southeastern seacoast, heartworm can now be found throughout the United States, and is transmitted through bites by mosquitoes. There are presently more than 60 species of mosquito known to transmit this illness. Heartworms spend their adult life attached to the right side of a dog's heart and the large blood vessels that attach the heart to the lungs. They can also be found in other species of animals but are rarely seen in humans.

Severely infected dogs can host several hundred adult heartworms which can live for five to seven years. This puts a very great strain on an infected dog's heart, which becomes enlarged, has to work harder, ages rapidly, and eventually weakens. Adult worms can obstruct the heart chambers and blood vessels between the heart and lungs. If a worm dies it can block the flow of blood to smaller vessels, thus causing any number of circulation-related problems. Symptoms include coughing, decreased appetite,

weight loss, and lethargy. In rare situations where infestations are very severe the dog may die of sudden heart failure.

The best way to deal with heartworms is to use preventive medications, but it is important to understand that these do not kill the adult worms. In addition, if preventives are used when adult heartworms are present, other severe problems can result, so it is very important to have your dog tested by your veterinarian for the presence of heartworms before any medications are started. If the fully grown worms are present, they need to be treated with an adulticide or through surgical procedures, which can become very difficult as the dying adults can cause obstructions in the bloodstream and/or embolisms.

There are a number of heartworm preventives available, and some will also help control other parasites. The two most popular are ivermectin and milbemycin. It is suggested that preventive medications should be used year round, even in areas where the mosquitoes occur seasonally. If given continuously, the preventive will stop the worms from developing into adults. The choice of medications should be discussed with your veterinarian so you can learn the pros and cons of each.

External Parasites

During the course of practically every dog's life, it will experience some form of discomfort that will be caused by external parasites, such as fleas, ticks, or mites. These parasites can be extremely irritating to pets (as well as their owners), and can cause serious skin problems. In addition, they can be the carriers of many diseases.

Fleas

The most common of canine parasites, fleas cause more pain and suffering than any other ailment. Fleas flourish when the weather turns warm and humid, so depending on the climate in which you live, fleas may be a seasonal or year-round problem. They differ from other parasites in that their strong hind legs enable them to jump long distances from one dog (or other mammalian host) to another. Adult fleas are dark brown and about the size of a sesame seed. They are highly mobile, and once they crawl under a dog's thick coat, they can move rapidly over their skin.

You may not know when your pet has a small infestation, but it is possible for 10 adult fleas to produce well over 250,000 offspring in 30 days, so if left untreated, it will be only a matter of time before your Cocker begins to show the obvious signs of discomfort. Symptoms of flea infestation range from mild redness of the skin to severe scratching that can lead to open sores and skin infections. Another sign of a flea infestation is the presence of small black flea "droppings" (about the size of fine, ground black pepper) that the parasite leaves on your pet's coat. The excrement is dried blood meal, so if you put some of the powder on a damp white tissue it will turn a rusty red-brown color as it dissolves. You may also see adult fleas, along with the excrement if you use a flea comb on an infested dog.

Fleas feed by biting their host and sucking their blood, so a Cocker with heavy flea infestations can become anemic. Some dogs are allergic to flea saliva, which results in even more irritation and scratching. Where infestations are very heavy, fleas have been known to bite humans.

With modern medicines, prevention of flea infestations is much easier and safer than it was in the past. There are several topical flea adulticides on the market today, (including imidacloprid and fipronil) that are very effective preventives. They do not require the flea to ingest blood, and can kill the flea before it bites, or lays eggs.

Ticks

These dangerous bloodsucking parasites can be found in just about all countries worldwide. They are of particular concern because some of them carry and transmit disease.

Tick populations and the diseases associated with them vary demographically. The *brown dog tick* is large enough to be seen with the human eye. While not all brown ticks are dangerous, this tick has been implicated as a carrier of Rocky Mountain Spotted Fever, and babesiosis. These two diseases have similar symptoms including fever, anorexia, depression, lethargy, and a rapid pulse rate. The *deer tick* is much smaller than the *brown dog tick*, and is

TIP

Tick Removal

You can remove ticks by carefully using tweezers to firmly grip the tick as close to the pet's skin as possible and gently pulling the tick free without twisting it. After removing the tick, you can crush it (while avoiding contact with fluids that can carry disease) or you can immerse it in a dilute solution of detergent or bleach.

If you live in an area where tick-borne diseases are known to occur, you can place the tick into a tightly sealed container and bring it to the veterinarian for examination. Do not attempt to smother the tick with alcohol or petroleum jelly, or apply a hot match to it, as this may cause the tick to regurgitate saliva into the wound and increase the risk of disease. Although humans cannot "catch" a tick-borne disease from an infected dog, they can become infected if they are bitten by a tick that is transmitting the disease.

barely perceptible to the human eye. It is this diminutive tick that is primarily responsible for the spread of Lyme disease.

Dogs that frequent grassy and wooded areas populated by wild mammals have the greatest risk exposure to ticks. Both the nymph and adult stages feed on animals. Unfed ticks resemble small crawling bugs, but once they attach themselves and begin to feed on their host, they begin to swell with blood until they look like a dried raisin, and as they continue to

gorge, a plump one. Ticks are most often found around a dog's neck, in the ears, in the folds between the legs and the body, and between the toes. Tick bites can cause skin irritation and heavy infestations can cause anemia. If you take your Cocker to tick-prone areas for fun or exercise, you should examine it for ticks immediately upon returning home and remove them from your pet. Prompt removal of ticks is very important because it lessens the chance of disease transmission. Pets at risk for ticks can be treated using preventive flea adulticides. Your veterinarian can recommend the product best suited to your needs.

Lice

Like most other external parasites, lice are bloodsuckers, and their bite causes irritation. They will spend their entire lives among the hair of their hosts. When they lay their eggs (called nits), they become firmly attached to the victim's hair. If your dog is infested you can see the egg clusters attached to the hairs. Lice can be very dangerous so bring your dog to the veterinarian if you spot eggs. Lice can be readily treated with insecticidal products.

Mites

These very small parasites do their damage by burrowing into a dog's skin, causing intense itching. Mites are no bigger than a pinhead, and require a microscope for proper identification. When they burrow into the skin in large numbers, they can cause a serious skin disease called mange. While mange can occur in healthy dogs, a clean sanitary environment is the best deterrent. This condition is more typically found in dogs that frequent unsanitary places and suffer from improper nutrition.

There are three principle forms of mites that infest dogs: ear mites, sarcoptic mange mites, and demodectic mange mites.

Ear mites are common in young dogs and generally confine themselves to the ear and surrounding areas. Ear mites can cause an intense irritation of the ear canal which can cause the infested dog to excessively shake his head or scratch his ears, sometimes to the point where bleeding sores are created. A black or brown ear discharge is another sign of ear mite infestations. This ailment can be treated by cleaning the ear and applying topical medications to the affected area.

Sarcoptic mange mites cause sarcoptic mange, also known as scabies. They are highly contagious and can be transmitted through close contact, bedding, or grooming tools. These mites burrow into the skin causing severe itching, hair loss, skin rashes, and crusting or scabbing of the affected areas. Infections can develop as a secondary result. People who come into close contact with an affected dog can develop skin rashes. Treatment of this ailment requires medication to kill the mites and additional treatments to relieve the itching and cure any infections. Cleaning and sanitizing the affected dog's environment is also necessary.

Demodectic mange mites are microscopic, and cause demodectic mange. This is not as contagious, but it can be passed from a mother to her puppies.

Unlike the other forms of mange, demodectic mange may indicate an underlying medical condition, so the victim's health must be carefully monitored, and treatment options will need to be discussed with your veterinarian.

A veterinarian can identify the type of mange in question by taking a skin sample and examining it under a microscope. Once the type of mange has been identified, the proper treatment can begin.

Common and Hereditary Ailments

I guess it should have been a warning when a veterinarian once said to me "I love Cocker Spaniels....they keep me busy." Well, truth be known, he was only partly kidding. Practically all purebred dogs have a predisposition for many diseases and ailments that are results of either poor breeding practices somewhere in the genealogy, or their anatomical structure. The Cocker Spaniel, unfortunately, is above average in the number of hereditary or higher-than-normal frequency conditions associated with a specific breed of dog.

It cannot be stressed enough that breeding practices (heredity), the environment, and socialization are all important factors in the health of an individual Cocker. Responsible breeders spend their lifetime building a quality bloodline, and certifying the health of their dogs. Some of the quality checks that Cocker Spaniel breeders attain for their dogs include O.F.A. (Orthopedic Foundation for Animals) testing for hip and elbow dysplasia, C.E.R.F. (Canine Eye Registration Foundation) certification for hereditary eye ailments, and BAER (Brainstem Auditory Evoked Response) Testing for congenital deafness.

Dogs shown to have any of the genetically linked ailments discussed here should not be used for breeding for fear of perpetuating the disease within the Cocker Spaniel bloodlines. Some are associated with both the English and American breeds, and some are associated with

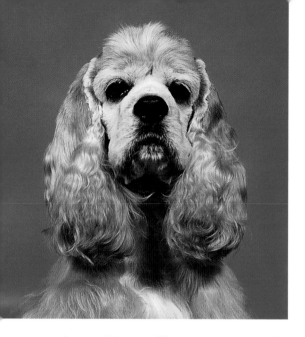

only one of the two. Ailments common to only one breed are noted as such.

Skin Disorders

Seborrhea and Dermatitis

These diseases both affect the dog's skin, and both may be related to dietary problems. Seborrhea is caused by the overproduction of sebaceous (oil) skin cells. The skin will appear greasy and scaly with a foul odor. It is normally seen on the posterior, back, and ears, and in extreme cases it can affect the whole body. Seborrhea can be successfully treated with the administration of retinoids (vitamin A derivatives). This therapy must be done under the guidance of a veterinarian as excessive amounts of vitamin A can have adverse reactions.

Dermatitis is a commonly occurring, inherited hypersensitivity to pollens or other environmental allergens (including food allergies) and is usually associated with a disorder of the Cocker's immune system. Symptoms of dermatitis include red dots, pimples, damp spots, crusty or scaly skin, and a loss of hair. The treatment for this ailment will vary, as the specific cause of the disease must first be identified.

Many times these skin disorders are the result of food allergies. The most common allergens in Cockers are beef, chicken, milk, eggs, corn, wheat, and soy. Many dogs that have food allergies also develop yeast and ear infections. When this happens, topical antifungal creams or ointments may be needed to treat the infection. Your veterinarian may also recommend a special shampoo and conditioner as well. Some Cocker owners have had much success in treating the symptoms using medicated oatmeal shampoo.

Lip Fold Dermatitis and Pyoderma

The skin on the lower jaw of the Cocker contains folds that characterize this breed. The dermatitis (inflammation) occurs when the folds trap moisture and/or undergo unusual rubbing. Many times this results in a bacterial infection, which is known as a pyoderma. These ailments are usually easy to manage by regular cleaning with a medicated cleaning agent and antibiotic therapy when an infection occurs. Treatment options should be discussed with your veterinarian. In chronic cases, the folds can be surgically removed.

Eye and Ear Disorders

Having such famous features as the Cocker's eyes and ears comes with a price. The following illnesses are all inherent in Cockers. While veterinarians may be very good at offering advice about these ailments, you may need to consider seeing an eye specialist.

Juvenile Cataracts and Glaucoma

Both of these hereditary conditions are very serious and if left untreated can lead to blindness. Cataracts form when the eye lens becomes cloudy or opaque, which causes the Cocker's vision to become blurred, and eventually lost. While old-age cataracts can be found in practically all breeds of dogs, they are not related to the juvenile form that can plague young dogs of genetically involved breeds. Juvenile cataracts come in two forms: the dissolving type where vision can be restored with cortisone eye drops, and the nondissolving type. Cockers that have the nondissolving form of juvenile cataracts will need to have an ophthalmologist determine if the retinas are normal before considering surgical removal of the cataract.

Glaucoma is caused by a fluid buildup that exerts abnormal amounts of pressure inside the eye. This tends to enlarge the eyeball causing much pain and possible blindness. Treatments for glaucoma also involve surgery as the medicinal treatments do not provide long-term control of the condition. These surgeries can be quite expensive, so it is very important that you get your dog from stock that has been shown to be free of hereditary eye problems.

Distichiasis

This genetically linked eye disorder is caused when a dog's eyelashes grow incorrectly and come into contact with the cornea, and are very irritating. Symptoms include squinting, excessive tearing, and inflammation. While electrolysis may be a temporary solution, surgery is usually required to permanently correct the problem.

Ectropion and Conjunctivitis

This hereditary eye condition is characterized by the abnormal growing or rolling out of the Cocker's lower eyelids, and appears to be more prevalent in the American breed. Ectropion allows the dog's fluid eye discharge to accumulate in the folds where it can lead to conjunctivitis, an eye infection that causes inflammation and keeps the dog's eye moist. In mild cases there may be no need for medical treatment, but usually this condition leads to chronic severe conjunctivitis. Ectropion indicates that the eyelid is too large, so it requires surgery to correct. Any associated conjunctivitis needs to be treated with topical medications.

Entropion

In this hereditary condition the eyelid rolls inward so the lashes and hair on the eyelid rub on the cornea. Entropion can cause severe corneal damage. This condition requires surgical treatment, which can be fairly simple and very effective. In severe cases the surgery can be much more involved and even require multiple procedures to correct the alignment.

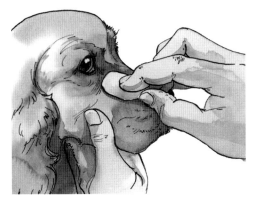

Clean your Cocker's eyes regularly.

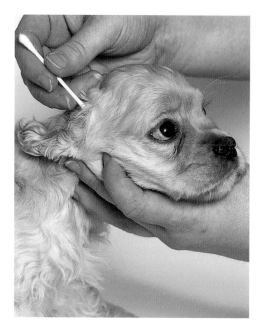

Retinal Dysplasia

This genetically linked eye ailment is the result of a malformed retina. The ailment is characterized by lesions on the retina that reduce the dog's vision. In severe cases the retina will become detached, which will cause blindness. This ailment can also lead to the secondary occurrence of cataracts or glaucoma. There is no cure for retinal dysplasia.

Progressive Retinal Atrophy (PRA)

This hereditary disease causes specialized dim light photoreceptors located in the retina to slowly deteriorate, which will lead to night blindness. As the disease progresses it will also lead to the deterioration of the bright light receptors as well, which results in complete blindness. There are no outward symptoms of this disease; it is characterized by a Cocker having difficulty seeing in the dark. Because of the slow progression, it is usually observed in dogs that are older than one year old. Unfortunately, there is no treatment for PRA, nor is there any therapy for slowing its progress.

Otitis

This ailment occurs in most dogs with long, pendulous ears. It is more common to the American than to the English Cocker. Otitis occurs when a dog's ear care is neglected and the buildup of moisture, dirt, wax, hair, and other foreign matter allows bacteria, yeasts, and molds to infect the external ear. The afflicted dog may hold one ear low (if only one ear is infected), scratch or rub his ear, shake his head, or cock his head at unusual angles. Often the ear will become reddened or inflamed, and sometimes there is a discharge of pusslike fluid from the ear canal. Otitis can be very difficult for your veterinarian to treat, and several re-treatments may be required. The best preventive measure is to make ear cleaning a regular part of your grooming schedule.

Congenital Deafness

This ailment is more common to the English Cocker, and is caused by a degeneration of the blood supply to the inner ear three to four weeks after birth. Dogs that suffer from this incurable hereditary disease will usually also have coats with a white pigmentation. It can affect one or both ears, and has no outward symptoms. Puppies afflicted with bilateral deafness (both ears) will fail to wake up when loud noises occur. A brainstem auditory-evoked response (BAER) test is used to diagnose deafness in dogs. Bilaterally deaf dogs are difficult to train and may develop behavioral problems as they are easily startled.

Autoimmune Disorders

Cockers seem to be more prone to autoimmune diseases than most other breeds. These disorders are extremely serious and can lead to fatalities in a matter of days.

Autoimmune Hemolytic Anemia (AIHA)

In AHIA, the Cocker's own immune system will attack its red blood cells. While the diagnosis can be made by your veterinarian during physical examination and blood testing, the cause is not always known. Symptoms include pale gums, fatigue, and sometimes jaundice (a yellowing of the skin). In severe cases the dog's liver may become enlarged and as a result, the abdomen will swell. Treatment includes steroid therapy, which helps to diminish the immune response, and some chemotherapy drugs. If too many red blood cells are lost, a transfusion may be necessary. While most forms of AIHA are treatable, death may still occur due to blood loss and related complications.

Skeletal Disorders

Hip Dysplasia

This inherited (and sometimes environmentally influenced) developmental disorder of the hip joints occurs most commonly in large breeds, but plagues the Cockers. The condition itself is due to a hip socket malformation that does not allow for the proper fit of the head of the femur.

At birth the hip of the afflicted dog appears normal, and signs of a problem may not be seen until the dog is at least five to nine months old. Hip dysplasia results in painful inflammation of the hip joint, which leads to permanent physical damage, including lameness and loss of the use of the back legs. Overfeeding, overexercising, and injury to a puppy may also contribute to a young Cocker damaging his hips.

Treatment for this ailment is to surgically correct the shape of the hip socket, or to perform a total hip replacement. Unfortunately, these surgeries (which have a very high success rate) are performed by only a small number of specialists, so they can be quite costly. If you are planning to breed your dog, be sure to have it certified free of hereditary hip dysplasia by the OFA.

Patellar Luxation

This condition is significantly more prevalent in the American breed. The patella (kneecap) is a small bone that guards a Cocker's knee joint. This bone sits in a groove in the femur, and is held in place by ligaments and muscles. Patellar luxation is a condition in which the bone can slide in and out of its proper position. The luxation can be hereditary or can be caused by injury, poor alignment, weak ligaments, or a malformation of the femur. Symptoms include limping, a hopping gate while running, or carrying the leg off the ground. In severe cases surgery may be required. Weight control is an important part of treating this disease (as well as hip dysplasia). Excessive weight will increase the strain on the joints, which can increase the level of discomfort and pain.

Overshot and Undershot Jaw

These genetically linked defects result from the dog's upper and lower jaws developing at different rates. Overshot jaws occur when the upper jaw grows too long for the lower jaw, and undershot jaws are the reverse. Sometimes puppies that have one of these conditions will grow out of it in time; however, puppies with a normal scissor bite can also develop an over- or undershot jaw as they mature. The true problem with this malformation is that it prevents the dog's teeth from lining up properly, so dogs with severe cases may have trouble picking up food and other objects, and misplaced canine teeth may press up against the gums or roof of the mouth. In these severe cases canine dentistry may be advised. This disorder would lead to disqualification in the show ring, so if you are looking for a show dog, be sure that this malady does not run in the bloodline.

Blood and Heart Disorders

Von Willebrand's Disease and X-Factor Deficiency

These inherited defects are both forms of hemophilia; a bleeding disorder caused by defective blood platelet function that does not allow the blood to clot properly. In addition to excessive or continuous bleeding from injuries, symptoms of these diseases include nosebleeds, bleeding from the gums, or blood in the urine or stool. X-Factor deficiency is more prevalent in the American Cocker, and all dogs in this breed should be tested for its presence. All Cocker breeds should be tested for the presence of von Willebrand's disease. It is extremely important for you and your veterinarian to know if your dog has a blood-clotting defect. If an afflicted dog becomes injured or requires surgery, the veterinarian will need to take special precautions. While there is no cure for the disease, several treatment options are available, and the choice is dependent upon the severity

of the disease. Treatments range from simply providing blood-clotting medications (such as vitamin K) in oral or intranasal form, to extensive plasma transfusions.

Patent Ductus Arteriosus (PDA)

Before birth, the blood flow of the fetus bypasses the lungs, which are not yet needed for breathing. Instead, blood flows from the right heart chambers to the left through the ductus arteriosus. At birth, pressure changes within the bloodstream should permanently close the duct, forcing blood to enter the lungs where oxygen can be exchanged. PDA is a failure to close the duct completely, allowing some blood to bypass the lungs. When this happens, even though the puppy is breathing, the proper amount of blood is not flowing to the lungs to meet the dog's oxygen needs.

Initially, no symptoms may be apparent, but as the puppy grows and the oxygen demands are not met, the dog will become less active, or may be short of breath and collapse, and the gums may appear to have a bluish tint. Your veterinarian may also be able to hear a turbulent blood flow with or without a stethoscope. Without surgical treatment, dogs suffering from PDA will most certainly live a shorter life than normal. The surgery has a high success rate and is best performed before the growth of the puppy is affected.

Other Health Problems

Hot Spots and Moist Eczema

This ailment, also known as summer sores, can appear anywhere on the body and spread rapidly. While hot spots can be caused by a variety of factors, the most common is bacteria. Any time the dog's skin becomes irritated and broken, it can become infected with bacteria, and when provided a moist environment (from baths, wet grass, licking, etc.) it offers the perfect conditions for the infection to spread. Hot spots do seem to be more prevalent in the summer, most likely because the hot weather will also promote bacterial growth. Hot spots can penetrate very deep into the skin, causing severe itching, which will cause the dog to scratch and lick excessively to relieve the pain, which only adds to the spread of the disease.

Hot spots that are bacterial in nature can be treated with oral or topical antibiotics. Because they can deeply penetrate the skin, keeping your dog well groomed and free of matting hair (or shaving the coat) will help to keep moisture from building up and reduce the occurrence and spread of hot spots during the summer. Providing your dog with a proper diet will help to keep his skin and coat in optimum condition, and reduce scratching that can lead to breaking the skin and then bacterial infection.

Constipation

As with humans, constipation in dogs is usually related to dietary issues. A lack of fiber or fresh water can disrupt your Cocker's digestive system, while ingesting foreign objects such as bones, rocks, or garbage can cause intestinal blockages. Constipation can also be caused by a lack of exercise, worm infestations, or medications that a dog may be taking.

The treatment used for constipation is dependent on the cause. If your dog is passing hard dry stools, then you can try adding fresh vegetables or $1/2$ teaspoon of bran to each meal to see if the stool softens. Make sure there is always plenty of fresh water available to drink, and exercise your dog an hour after each meal. In chronic cases or severe cases, or when you know that the cause is the ingestion of a foreign object then you should bring your dog to a veterinarian immediately.

Shock

This condition is caused by a lack of blood flow to meet the body's needs, so any condition that adversely affects the heart or blood volume can induce shock. It can be brought on by hemorrhages, poisoning, and dehydration, but in dogs the most common cause is being hit by a car. The symptoms of shock, which are the result of inadequate blood circulation, are a drop in body temperature, shivering, listlessness, depression, weakness, cold feet and legs, and a weakened pulse.

If your dog is in shock, keep him calm and speak to him in a soft reassuring voice. If the shock is caused by blood loss from an open wound, then you will need to control the bleeding (discussed later in this chapter). Let your dog get into a comfortable position that causes the least amount of pain and makes breathing easier. Cover the dog with a blanket or a coat (but not too tightly) to keep him warm. Because the actions of a dog in shock can be unpredictable, you need to use caution when handling it. As they are small dogs, a sick or injured Cocker can be carried, but a blanket "stretcher" can also be used to transport him. When possible, splint or support broken bones before moving your dog, and carry him with the injured parts protected. Use a muzzle only when absolutely necessary as it can impair the

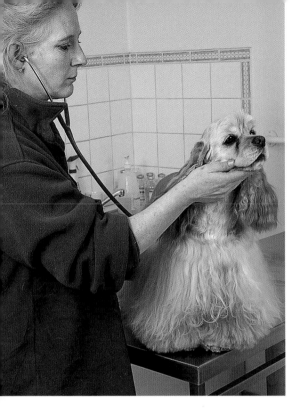

used will depend on the severity of the injury, the type of bone that is broken, and the age of the Cocker. Growing puppies heal faster than geriatric dogs, so your veterinarian may decide to use a cast on a puppy, but use pins for the same injury to an older dog.

Poisoning

Humans and dogs live their lives surrounded by poisons and toxins; however, dogs cannot read warning labels, which puts them at an extreme disadvantage. Most cases of poisoning are the result of ingestion, although a few may be caused by other forms of exposure such as inhalation. Unfortunately, despite the best intentions of their owners, poisoning is common in dogs due to their curious nature and indiscriminate diets. The amount of damage a poison does to its victim is related to the amount the dog ingests (or inhales), and how long it has been in the body before treatment. If treatment is immediate, some poisons may not cause any significant illness. Some, regardless of the speed at which they are treated can be fatal or result in permanent damage.

The effects of a poison may not always be immediately seen. Some will not cause illness for days or weeks after exposure, but most common poisons result in symptoms that can be seen within three or four days after exposure. Because of this time lapse, you should never wait to see any symptoms when you see your dog ingesting a potentially harmful substance. If you see your Cocker ingest a potentially harmful substance, read the label for warnings and the proper therapy or antidote you should use. You can also call your veterinarian and/or poison control center (whose

dog's breathing, and bring him immediately to a veterinarian.

Broken Bones

Fractures and broken bones are also frequently the result of auto accidents. A dog with a fracture will be in severe pain, so approach him with caution, as he may attempt to bite. If the dog has a compound fracture (where the broken bone has punctured the skin), cover the wound with gauze or a clean cloth to prevent infection, and bring the injured dog to a veterinarian, as soon as possible. Any fracture, simple or compound, requires professional attention.

Just as in humans, your veterinarian will use splints, casts, steel plates, and screws to realign the bone and allow it to heal. The treatment number you should always have by your telephone), for the recommended course of treatment. Taking immediate action can sometimes mean the difference between life and death, so there may be times when you will need to take some action yourself. Also, report all cases of toxic ingestion to your veterinarian as soon as possible.

Some of the most common poisons found in most peoples homes include antifreeze, acetaminophen, pesticides, lead, and rodent poisons. Fortunately, most of these have known antidotes, but not all poisons do, so keep all potentially harmful substances away from your pets, and be sure your pets are not located in the same area when you are using them.

Bleeding Wounds

As discussed earlier, excessive bleeding can cause shock, so all pet owners should know how to stop a hemorrhage if their pet is injured. This is especially true for the owners of hunting dogs who have a greater risk of deep puncture wounds from hidden wood shards or wire, and are far away from immediate veterinary treatment. If you plan to hunt with your Cocker, be sure your first aid kit includes everything you need for the dogs as well. The following techniques used to stop external bleeding are given in their order of preference.

✔ *Direct pressure* can be applied by gently pressing a gauze or clean cloth compress over the bleeding area. The compress is used to absorb the blood and allow it to clot. Do not disturb the clot once it has formed; if the blood seeps through, put another compress over it and continue the direct pressure more evenly. Once the bleeding is controlled, use bandage material to hold the compress in place so you can take other emergency actions. If no compress is available, you can use your bare hand or a finger.

✔ *Elevation* of a severely bleeding foot or leg wound so that it is above the level of the heart uses the force of gravity to help reduce blood pressure and slow the bleeding. It should be used in conjunction with direct pressure to be effective in stopping the bleeding. If the bleeding continues, you will need to apply finger or thumb pressure on the supplying artery. Use the femoral artery (in the groin) for bleeding in the rear legs, the brachial artery (in the inside upper front leg) for the forelegs, or the caudal artery (at the base of the tail) if the wound is on the tail. Continue applying direct pressure.

✔ *Pressure above and below the bleeding wound* can also be used in conjunction with direct pressure. Pressure above the wound will help control arterial bleeding while the pressure applied below the wound will help control bleeding from the veins.

✔ *Tourniquets* can be very dangerous, and should therefore be used only for a severe, life-threatening wound to the leg or tail, which is not expected to be saved. Use a 2-inch-wide (5-cm-wide) piece of cloth to wrap twice around the limb, above the wound, and tie it into a half-knot. Take a short stick, place it over the half-knot, and tie the other half of the knot. Twist the stick to tighten the tourniquet until the bleeding stops, then secure it in place with another piece of cloth and make a note of the time it is applied. Loosen the tourniquet for 15-20 seconds every 20 minutes. Remember that using a tourniquet can be very dangerous and will likely result in the loss of the limb, so use it only as a last resort.

Nursing a Sick Dog

In order to determine if your Cocker is ill, or if you are taking care of a convalescing pet, there are several procedures you will need to monitor and understand the condition of your pet's health, and assure a speedy recovery.

Taking the Temperature

To determine if your dog has a fever, you will need to take the dog's temperature, which is relatively easy; all you need is a thermometer (and petroleum jelly if you are taking a rectal temperature). A Cocker's normal rectal temperature is 100.5 to 101.5°F (38 to 38.6°C), which may be slightly higher in younger dogs, and slightly lower in older ones. Some dogs do not like having their rectal temperatures taken, while others do not seem to mind. If you have a dog that struggles when you try to take his temperature rectally, you may want to consider using an ear thermometer, which is fast and easy, but must be used properly to get an accurate reading.

To take a rectal temperature wait until your dog is placid. Then with a quick shake of the thermometer, get the reading below 99°F (37.2°C), lubricate the end with KY or petroleum jelly, and slip the thermometer into the dog's rectum (located just below the base of its tail). Keep it there for two or three minutes (or until a digital thermometer beeps). If your dog is resistant, you can hold his head in the crook of one arm leaving your other arm free to insert the thermometer. If your dog is very resistant, you can seek the help of another person to hug the head and front part of the dog, while you take his temperature. Be sure to properly clean the thermometer after each use. Clean glass thermometers with alcohol and

store. Store digital thermometers according to the manufacturer's instruction.

The normal ear temperature for a Cocker Spaniel is 100°F to 103.0°F (37.8°C to 39.4°C); an ear thermometer works by measuring infrared heat waves coming from the eardrum area. This is considered a good area to use because it measures brain blood temperature. To do this you will need an ear thermometer that is made for dogs, because they have a longer probe arm that is designed for a canine ear. Lift your Cocker's ear flap, and place the thermometer deep into the horizontal ear canal to obtain an accurate reading. The first several times you use it you should also take a rectal reading and compare the results. They should be very close if you are using the right technique.

If your dog has a temperature of less than 99°F (37.2°C) or greater than 104°F (40°C), contact your veterinarian.

Taking a Pulse

There are several areas on your Cocker's body where you should be able to feel a pulse, which occurs every time the heart beats. Sometimes you can place your hands low on the dog's chest, near the elbow joint and feel the heart beat. The second place to find the pulse is on the inner side of the thigh (near where the hind leg meets the torso). Here you will be feeling for the femoral artery. Use two fingers (index and middle) in this location to feel for the femoral pulse. An adult Cocker has a pulse rate of 75 to 95 beats per minute. Puppies will have a faster pulse, which may be as high as 160 beats per minute.

In a calm and healthy dog the pulse is strong but it may not always be steady. Normally the pulse rate will change as the dog breathes in or

TIP

Giving Medication Directly

If you need to use force to get a dog to take his medications you can use the following. Get the pill out, hold it with your thumb and index finger, and call the dog with a happy voice. Place the dog's hind end against a wall so it cannot back away from you. Using your other hand, gently grasp the dog's muzzle from the top with the thumb on one side and the fingers on the other. Squeeze behind the upper canine teeth and tilt the head back to automatically open its mouth. Use one finger, on the hand holding the pill, to push down between the lower canine teeth, and place the pill as far back into the dog's mouth as possible, making sure to get it over the "hump" of the tongue. Close the dog's mouth and hold it closed, lower the head into a normal position, and gently rub or blow on the

dog's nose to help stimulate it to swallow. When you are done, be sure to give the patient plenty of praise and a treat if his diet allows, which will make it easier to do the next time. You can also ask your veterinarian to show you how it is done, because seeing a live demonstration is a great way to learn.

Giving your dog liquid or oral syringe medications can be given in much the same way as a pill. Be sure to shake the medicine and have it measured in a syringe or eyedropper before you call the dog. Once the mouth is open, place the tip of the syringe or eyedropper into the pocket formed between the dog's cheek and back teeth, and slowly administer the medication, with slight pauses to allow the dog to swallow it.

out (faster on inhalation, and slower on exhalation). While this is normal behavior, a weak pulse may indicate poisoning, while an irregular pulse is a symptom of an infection.

Administering Medication

In order for a dog to properly recover from illnesses, it is very important that they receive their medications and ingest the correct dosage for oral preparations. If you are lucky your dog may take his medicine directly from your hand, but sometimes when the patient is unwilling, you need to find another way. If your dog is not on a restricted diet, you can

hide his pills in a small amount of peanut butter, cream cheese, or sandwich meat. Do not mix medications in your dogs regular meal. It is important that the entire dose be consumed at one time, so if the dog eats only half its food, he will not have gotten the proper dosage.

Home Care for the Older Cocker

As a dog ages, he will experience a gradual decline in his physical and sometimes mental capabilities. Small breeds like the Cocker Spaniel usually are considered geriatric between nine and thirteen years old. Like humans, geriatric dogs require special care from their owners, to help minimize the effects of the aging process, and make their golden years as comfortable as possible.

Make sure that your pet's living and sleeping space is clean, warm, and protected. You should provide soft bedding, and limit the changes to the dog's environment, including prolonged changes in temperatures that many geriatric dogs cannot adjust well to. Older dogs may also have a harder time seeing, so be careful about placing new or potentially dangerous objects in locations where your dog usually moves. You can also consider stomping your feet as you approach your lounging dog to give him a warning of your presence. Should your older Cocker experience stiffening joints or arthritis, you should avoid picking him up unnecessarily, and you may need to consider building ramps that will provide easier access to your home. You can also consult with your veterinarian about using nonsteroidal anti-inflammatory drugs (NSAID), such as ibuprofen, for relief of arthritic pain.

- Groom your Cocker, and be sure to brush his teeth regularly, and provide him with the exercise an aging dog still needs to stay in peak health. Grooming helps promote healthy skin and coat, and gives the owner the opportunity to perform a home health exam.
- Check the dog's teeth and mouth for any dental problems or foul odors.
- Feel the skin for lumps, and look for skin sores or discharges from the eyes and ears.
- Feel the Cocker's limbs and abdomen for swelling or signs of pain.

Unless otherwise directed by your veterinarian, routine exercise is very important to the geriatric Cocker. Walk your dog as often as possible. Even if the dog does not walk well, a short daily walk will help improve his circulation, stimulate the heart muscles, and the change in environment will provide some mental stimulation.

Be sure that your older dog always has access to fresh, clean water. If your Cocker is having trouble getting up, it may become necessary for you to bring the water dish to your pet. If your dog does have trouble moving, be extra careful about exposing him to extreme weather, as he may have trouble getting out of the sun, or finding a warm corner when the weather gets colder. In these cases you will need to either keep the dog inside, or be sure adequate shelter is nearby. In addition, dogs that have trouble moving or problems with their eyesight should not be left in elevated locations, such as on a table, couch, or stair, where they could injure themselves trying to get down.

Be careful not to let the older, less active dog become overweight. Feed your aging Cocker a good-quality diet that is appropriate for his aging and medical needs. Avoid giving too many treats, as these can lead to the gaining of unnecessary weight. If your dog always had free access to food, you may need to switch to a once- or twice-a-day program to better monitor food intake. If your dog has teeth problems, it may become necessary to soften his food by adding water to allow hard kibble to soften. Be sure to discuss all instances of unexpected weight gain (or loss) with your veterinarian, who may recommend a specific diet.

As your dog becomes older, you will need to pay even more attention to the indicators of health. Symptoms such as irregular breathing, excessive panting, bouts of whining, weakness in the rear legs are all signs that you need to discuss with your veterinarian. Providing a good home and proper veterinary care can definitely help your Cocker live a longer, happier life.

Saying Good-bye

During the course of dog ownership there is no more difficult decision you may have to make as when your loving and loyal friend has become terminally ill and will soon die. While modern veterinary medicine has many ways to extend the life of our pets, there comes a point where veterinary care will no longer serve a useful purpose. If your dog becomes terminally ill and is experiencing severe and constant pain, aggressive medical attention will not extend its life but instead it prolongs the dying process. Euthanasia is the act by which a veterinarian painlessly induces death, ending the suffering of a terminally ill animal. When the time comes you must be ready to consider your pet's feelings as well as your own. This is never an easy choice, but it has been made in the past by millions of pet owners who also loved their pets.

There is no universal process that will help every pet owner through the euthanasia process, and the grief that follows is a different experience for everyone. The most loving and caring of dog owners can become cold and callous, while strong objective owners may completely fall apart. This is a personal experience, where *you* need to decide what is best for you and your pet.

Most pet owners experience a strong and lasting sense of grief and loss after the passing of their beloved pets. Part of the problem arises because there is no one available who can relate to the personal bond that forms between a dog and his master, and part is

because many people feel that talking about it will make them the subject of ridicule. The bereavement of a loving pet owner can often be self-critical and may even bring up memories of other losses in one's personal life. This can lead to sadness, helplessness, and even clinical depression. There is nothing wrong with feeling this way and as a loving, caring pet owner, there is no need to apologize for it. If you feel the need to talk to someone who understands, there are a number of support groups that specialize in pet loss counseling. Never feel ashamed or belittle yourself for the strong feelings you felt for your pet, and know that you are not alone. You can look for these support groups on the Internet, or ask your veterinarian for the telephone number of your local Veterinary Medical Association, to be directed to the nearest pet loss specialist.

BASIC AND ADVANCED TRAINING

Like most hunting dogs, the Cocker Spaniel is relatively easy to train. Because of several hundred years of close hunter-dog relationships, the Cocker has an innate willingness to learn. For this reason you can begin to train your Cocker at an earlier age than is possible with many other breeds. Likewise, the Cocker's acquired hunting-dog attentiveness will permit longer training sessions, thus leading to quicker learning.

Setting Up a Good Program

While it is possible to teach your Cocker just about anything, this chapter deals primarily with the basic lessons that every dog should know, as well as some of the fundamental exercises for the prospective gundog.

Bear in mind that, while every Cocker has the ability to learn and perform these exercises, it is up to you, her master, to teach the lessons properly. This instruction will take time, energy, and patience. Your puppy will depend on you to find the right method to teach her. Once this method is established, however, your Cocker will respond both eagerly and joyfully.

Cockers are a unique and entertaining breed to train because, while they are rapid and attentive learners, they are also opportunists and will try to take advantage of every break they are given. For instance, if you are not firm enough in your commands, your dog may pretend that she did not hear you and go on with whatever activity she chooses. If you should then get upset and yell, she will find a way to punish you for injuring her pride. One of my Cockers, before obeying my commands, would run around or under every jumping hurdle until she finally got me to smile and laugh. Once that was done, she began to perform as expected.

I have found from experience that Cockers can be trained much more easily by using smiles and encouragement rather than anger and physical force. Therefore, if you are in the middle of a training session and your student's attention starts to wander, or if you feel you are being ignored, consider ending the lesson early and reviewing the rules of training. When you find out what the problem was, be sure to correct it in your next session.

Training a Puppy

Teaching a Puppy Her Name

Presumably, you will have chosen a name for your puppy before picking her up. Therefore, the first lesson, teaching your puppy her name, will actually begin the moment you leave the breeder's house. This is one of the easiest lessons to teach, for all you do is address your puppy by name each time you talk to her. You will be amazed at how fast the puppy will learn this lesson. Just be sure to use the same name all the time and to avoid the urge to use nicknames, which will only lead to confusion.

The Word "No"

The next important lesson to teach your Cocker puppy is the word "no." There is little doubt that you will have ample opportunity to teach this lesson in the first few days the puppy is in your home. Whenever you see her

do something wrong, say "No" in a sharp, firm tone that shows you are serious. If the puppy refuses to listen, pick her up and place her in her cage. Remember never to use force, which will only make the puppy hand-shy.

Using a cage will simplify training in general and can be a tremendous aid in housebreaking a puppy.

Walking on a Leash

This is another lesson that should begin as soon as you bring your puppy home. Each time you take your Cocker out to relieve herself or to exercise her, you should put on her collar (making sure it is neither too tight nor too loose) and attach a leash of sufficient length. As you walk, hold the leash on your left side and use gentle persuasion to keep the puppy close to your leg. Do not allow the puppy to get under your feet or to run ahead of you. Remain patient. A Cocker puppy's legs are very short, and she is not capable of tremendous speed. If your puppy falls behind, do not attempt to drag her forward. Use friendly words, patience, and, if necessary, a tiny bit of gentle physical persuasion to keep your puppy in her proper walking position.

Obedience Training

Obedience training is extremely important, and the basic exercises should be learned by every dog. Even if you decide not to enter your dog in an obedience trial, these lessons will help you to handle your dog properly in awkward situations and may even help save your

You should begin to train your puppy to walk on a leash as soon as you bring her home.

Basic Rules of Training

The ten rules listed here will help to set up a good training program for your Cocker puppy. Each time you begin a training session make sure you adhere to these rules. This will assure that you are giving your puppy the best chance to learn her lessons as thoroughly and rapidly as possible.

1. Begin working with your puppy the day you bring her home. Hold two or three sessions a day and hold them for as long as the puppy shows interest. In 10 or 15 minutes you can provide sufficient teaching without boring the dog. Your puppy may need two weeks or longer to begin understanding some of your commands, so do not neglect your training.

2. Be consistent. All of the members of your household must decide what is permitted behavior and what is not. For instance, one person should not be teaching the dog to "beg" for food, while the others are teaching the dog not to hang around the dinner table. Once your dog has learned a lesson, never allow her to do the contrary without a reprimand.

3. Be authoritative. Your dog will understand tones better than words. You must deliver all visual and verbal commands clearly and unmistakably. Reprimands must be sharp and firm while praise is calm and friendly. While the dog must learn that you are in charge, never demonstrate your authority by using physical force. In addition to being totally unnecessary, forcing your dog to perform, or hitting her, will only teach your dog to dislike her training sessions.

4. Hold each training session in an atmosphere conducive to learning. Be sure there are as few distractions as possible, and never attempt to teach your puppy anything when

you are in a bad mood. Your negative attitude will only confuse the puppy and make learning harder.

5. Do not attempt to teach your puppy more than one new lesson in a single session, and never move onto a new concept until the dog has mastered the previous one. Puppies, like people, learn at their own pace and should never be rushed. Once a lesson has been mastered, it can be included as a warm-up exercise in your dog's training regimen.

6. Praise your dog generously for her successes. Verbal praise, petting, or scratching behind the ears will make your Cocker an eager student. Although it is commonplace for trainers to reward their pupils with food, this practice is not necessary. Enthusiastic praise should be enough incentive for your puppy to perform correctly.

7. Punish disobedience immediately. Because a puppy has a very short memory, you must never put off a reprimand. If, for example, your puppy chews a slipper, do not punish her unless you catch her in the act; otherwise she will not understand why you are displeased. An adult dog that knows better, however, can be disciplined for the same offense after showing it the slipper.

8. Limit punishments to verbal reprimands. In extreme cases, you can confine your dog to her cage after giving her a verbal reprimand.

9. Even when your dog is older, keep your training sessions short, and end them early if the dog begins to lose interest.

10. Never hold a training session when your dog is tired; a tired or exhausted dog will not be attentive. Make it a practice to hold your training sessions before you feed your Cocker, as she will be less likely to be sleepy or sluggish.

pet from harm. All of the lessons in this group can be taught to your dog at home. However, if you prefer to seek the services of an expert dog handler, you can sign your Cocker up for obedience classes.

Obedience schools provide the proper atmosphere for teaching your dog all she must learn to compete in shows, as well as how she should act in the world of humans, and offer an interesting and easy alternative to training your dog yourself. You may wish to have an older child in your household take the dog to these classes. In this way the child and the dog can spend more time together and the child learns the responsibilities of proper pet care.

A list of reputable obedience schools in your area can be obtained from your local Cocker club or the AKC. Before enrolling your dog, however, make sure that the class suits your purpose. Some schools have special classes for show-dog handling as well as sessions designed for amateurs.

Basic Commands

The first three commands to teach your puppy are *sit, stay,* and *come.* To make it easy for your Cocker to recognize these commands, you should keep them short and simple: for example, *"Sit"* or *"Sit, Millie"* instead of *"Sit over there, Millie."* While dogs are fairly smart, they do not understand complete sentences; instead they rely on hearing the command word and interpreting your tone of voice and body gestures.

Sit: Take your puppy into an isolated room and fit her with a collar and leash. Holding the leash with your right hand, place your left hand on the puppy's hindquarters. Then give the command *"Sit!"* or *"Sit, Millie!"* in a firm voice, at the same time pressing gently and steadily on the dog's hindquarters. Gently pull the leash upward to keep your puppy from lying down on the floor. Hold the dog in this position for a while; do not allow her to jump back up.

Repeat the procedure until the session ends or until the puppy begins to lose interest. Remember to praise your Cocker each time she sits properly, but do not expect her to master this command perfectly in the first training session.

Once your puppy has performed the *sit* at least a couple of times in succession, remove the leash and give the command. If your dog does not perform correctly, remain patient and try again with the leash on. Repetition and consistency are the keys to teaching this lesson. With proper training it should not take very long for your Cocker to master this command.

If you plan on entering your Cocker in field trials or are considering using her as a hunting

*In teaching the **sit** command, use one hand to gently push the hindquarters down, and the leash to keep the dog's head upright.*

dog, you should teach her to respond to hand signals and whistles as well as the spoken word. In the field, your Cocker may be at a distance where she cannot clearly hear your commands, but can see gestures or hear the sharp, piercing sound of a whistle. Thus, even at a distance you can still have some control over your dog. Once your dog has mastered the command, hold up either your entire hand or a single finger in a distinct gesture and say *"Sit,"* making sure the dog can see the signal. Always use the word (or sound) and the gesture together so that your dog connects the two.

Stay: This command is usually more difficult to teach because your puppy will always want to be at your side, and *stay* orders your dog to remain wherever she is. However, this command may someday save your dog's life, should she start to run into a busy street.

In teaching your dog the *stay,* first fit her with a leash and collar. Then run through the *sit* procedure, and follow it with the command *"Stay."* As you say this new command, raise your hand, palm toward the dog, like a police officer stopping traffic. Each time your dog attempts to stand up, reproach it with a sharp *"No!"*

Take up all the slack in the leash to hold your student in place, and repeat the procedure until the dog appears to understand. Then remove the leash and repeat the command several times. Praise the dog each time she obeys, and reprimand disobedience.

Continue this command until your Cocker has repeated the act with consistent success. Then slowly back away from the dog, making sure to

Use the proper hand signal when teaching. In this case the Cocker will associate a flat, open-handed gesture with the stay command.

maintain eye contact. As you move backward, keep repeating *"Stay."* If your Cocker attempts to follow, utter a loud, sharp *"No!"* If the dog continues forward, reprimand her. Naturally a dog that stays when told deserves lavish praise.

Come: Although for the most part your puppy will race to you when you call her name, the trick to the *come* command is to have your Cocker come to you obediently when something of greater interest is attracting her attention. You should teach the *come* command to your puppy right after *sit* and *stay.* Start by running through the procedures for these two commands. Once your puppy has stayed at a good distance, call the dog by name (for example, *"Millie"*) and follow with the command *"Millie, come."* Accompany your words with a lively sound or gesture, such as clapping your hands or slapping your thighs, to help excite your dog into motion.

Your little student will quickly associate the word *"Come"* with your movements. Praise her for responding correctly. If she does not respond to the command, put the puppy on a long rope

and let her wander off. Then slowly reel in the rope while repeating the word *"Come!"* Shower your dog with praise when she reaches you. Repeat this exercise several times, then try it without the rope again. While using a rope may seem drastic, it is important that your Cocker master this exercise, for, like *stay,* the *come* command can help protect your dog from accidents.

Heeling

Heeling is a mandatory skill for Cockers entered in obedience trials. When your dog heels properly, she will walk on your left with her head about the same distance forward as your knees. When you begin teaching your dog this lesson, you will require a leash. Eventually, though, your Cocker must learn to heel without the restraint of the leash.

To start, run through all the other commands your dog has mastered. Successful performance will give your dog extra confidence before you start this difficult lesson. Hold the end of the leash in your right hand, and grab about halfway toward the collar with your left hand. Begin a brisk walk, giving the sharp command *"Heel!"* and using your left hand to control and guide.

If your dog lags behind, pull gently on the leash to bring her even with your leg. Do not drag the dog forward or force her to obey your commands, lest you destroy the well-established learning atmosphere. If your dog runs forward, pull her back to your side and give the *heel* command again.

If you have difficulty getting your dog to perform correctly, run through the *sit* and *stay* exercises. Once again, praise successes and reprimand disobedience. When the *sit* and the *stay* have been performed correctly, begin *heel* exercises again.

The *heel* lesson is very difficult for a dog to learn, so take your time and be patient. Once the *heel* command on a leash has been mastered, take your student through a turning exercise. If she has trouble heeling while you turn, take a shorter grip on the leash, and bring the dog closer to your side. Then repeat the command *"Heel!"* in a sharp tone, and gently persuade your puppy to follow you by lightly pulling on the leash. As your Cocker gains confidence, take her through a series of straight line, right turn, and left turn exercises.

Once your pet has mastered turning, it is time to begin training with a slack leash. Go through the *heel* exercise with the leash exerting no pressure on your dog's collar. At the first mistake, grasp the leash firmly and lead the dog steadily in the proper direction. When she performs correctly, praise her generously.

When your dog has learned to walk correctly with a slack leash, remove the leash completely. If your puppy has performed with a loose leash, you should be able to achieve the same results without a leash, provided that you do not change your routine. Continue to praise or reprimand as warranted. If you have trouble, you will have to put the leash back on and repeat the lesson.

Keep in mind that the *heel* is very difficult to master. If you are patient and persistent, however, your dog will eventually learn her lesson.

Lying Down

Have your Cocker assume a sitting position, and then slowly pull her front legs forward while saying *"Down!"* If your dog attempts to stand up, give her a sharp *"No!"* If necessary, push down on the dog's shoulders at the same time that you pull her front legs slowly forward. While you do this, give the command *"Down!"* Because you will have both hands occupied, you should carefully step on the leash to prevent the dog from returning to her feet. Keep the dog in the lying position for about one minute, and gradually increase this time period as your dog progresses.

When your pupil has mastered this lesson, begin to move away, while maintaining constant eye contact. Whenever the dog attempts to stand up, repeat the command *"Down!"* in a firm, sharp tone. Continue the lessons until you are satisfied with the results, and remember to praise your puppy for each successful performance.

Training for Hunting Dogs

While the skills described in this section are all required in the obedience ring, they are also desirable for a hunting dog. These exercises can be difficult for a Cocker to master, so be patient and understanding.

Relinquishing an Object

Every dog must be taught to give up any object, no matter how desirable, on command. For hunting dogs it is doubly important that they relinquish their prey as soon as their master tells them to do so. For training purposes, you can substitute a piece of nonsplintering wood for a downed woodcock.

Give your Cocker the wood to hold in her teeth. Then command your dog to sit, praising her when she obeys. Using both hands, slowly pull the dog's jaws apart, while saying, *"Let go!"* in a strict, firm tone. If your dog begins to growl, give her a sharp *"No!"* Do not be afraid if your Cocker growls. This is a dog's way of trying to establish its dominance, and a natural reaction to anyone who attempts to seize her

prey. You must, however, make it clear to your dog that you are the boss by taking the object away. Once your dog accepts you as a dominant force, she will give up the wood without any objection.

Retrieving

Retrieving is a skill that can be taught fairly easily to most Cockers. In fact, a properly trained hunting Cocker must flush the game, drop into a sitting position so as not to interfere with the shot, and retrieve on command only. This procedure also includes retrieval from water.

Start by throwing a suitably sized, nonedible ball or stick, with your dog standing next to you, and call out, *"Fetch!"* If the dog picks up the object in her mouth and returns to you, command your pet to sit, put your hand, palm up, under her jaw, and say, *"Let go!"* You should be able to remove the object from the dog's mouth without any resistance. If your dog drops the object, place it back in her mouth, and then remove it, saying *"Let go!"*

If your Cocker fails to return with the object, repeat the exercise using a 30-foot (9-m) rope. Tie the dog to the rope, throw the object, and call out, *"Fetch!"* again. Once the Cocker has picked up the object, draw the dog toward you and then take the object from her.

If your dog hesitates to pick up the object, place the object in her mouth and follow the commands in the preceding section for relinquishing an object. Keep repeating this lesson until the dog understands that this object is to be taken into her mouth. Then throw the object a short distance to see whether the dog will pick it up.

Jumping over Hurdles

Jumping over hurdles is sometimes difficult for a Cocker to master. However, a hunting dog must learn to leap over obstacles that separate her from downed prey. First, command your dog to sit on one side of a small pile of boards of reasonable height, while you stand on the opposite side. Then command the dog by saying *"Jump!"* If she walks around the obstacle, say *"No!"* and then bring her back and start over. Be sure to praise your dog for a successful performance.

As your dog learns to jump over the hurdle on command, gradually increase the obstacle's height. Be careful, however, not to make the jump too high, lest your young dog be injured and discouraged from further jumping.

Once your dog has learned to jump on command, begin a jump and retrieve exercise. Place the object to be retrieved on the other side of the hurdle, and command your dog to sit next to you. Then command it to retrieve the object by saying, *"Jump! Fetch!"* in a clear, firm voice. The dog should leap over the obstacle, pick up the object, and jump back with it. Tell the dog to sit again, and take the object out of her mouth while saying, *"Let go!"* Finally, praise your dog warmly for her accomplishment.

Tips for Training Older Dogs

As I mentioned earlier, the purpose of training dogs when they are young is to teach them how they are expected to behave before any bad habits can form. For the most part, training an older dog consists primarily of breaking any bad habits she may have picked up that prevent her from accomplishing your goals. These habits may have resulted from failure to observe any one of the rules of training and, once established as part of the dog's behavior, may require drastic action to eliminate.

Bad Habits

The first step is to analyze the situation in order to find out, if possible, how the bad habit was formed. For example, a dog that barks excessively may, as a puppy, have been given a reward of food each time she performed the *speak* command correctly. As a result, the dog may bark whenever she is hungry or wants a treat. Thus, the best way to correct this behavior is to make sure that the dog is *never* rewarded with food when she barks on command. This method, termed "extinction," calls on the trainer to repeat the *speak* command over and over, but never, ever to give a reward except verbal praise and petting.

Bad habits can also be broken by using punishment. The punishment, however, should never include hitting or throwing things at the dog. Instead, each time your dog performs the undesirable conditioned act, it should be scolded with a sharp *"No!"* If the problem persists, the punishment should be confinement to the cage. Once again, the key to success is to scold or confine the dog every time she exhibits the bad habit. This method works particularly well for breaking nasty habits such as begging or excessive barking and can also be used to control an overaggressive dog.

Solving Training Problems

Every Cocker Spaniel can master all of the commands and exercises discussed in this chapter. Should your Cocker turn out to be a slow learner, be patient, persistent, and understanding. If you display these qualities in your teaching, eventually your dog's training will become complete.

If your dog shows an unwillingness to learn, or seems to be having trouble with a particular lesson, examine your teaching methods. Review the section entitled "Setting Up a Good Program" and the "Basic Rules of Training" and go over each of these basic rules. Ask yourself whether you have followed these precepts during all of your sessions. Once you have identified the problem, you should correct it immediately.

If, however, after thoroughly reviewing your methods, you feel that your instruction is not the problem, carefully consider your dog and its environment. Could your Cocker possibly be distracted by an outside factor? If so, remove the distraction. Could your dog be ill? If an ailment is suspected, make an appointment with your veterinarian.

Finally, should you continue to run into training difficulties, I strongly recommend that you contact a reputable obedience school. The professional dog handlers who run obedience facilities can usually diagnose and correct problems rather easily.

If you start early and work hard, be assured that your Cocker can be trained to whatever stage you desire.

Cocker Spaniels in Competition

Many Cocker owners are attracted to participating in dog shows because it combines the excitement of competition with a chance to spend more quality time with their dogs. In the United States the AKC sponsors many events, attracting millions of participants. These events include conformation shows, obedience trials, field trials, hunting tests, agility trials, Canine Good Citizen tests, lure coursing, herding trials, and tracking tests. While Cocker Spaniels can compete in many of these events, they are most commonly found competing in conformance shows, obedience trials, and the field trials and hunting tests that are designed for dogs that have been bred as hunting companions.

Should you decide to try the show ring, keep in mind that no individual dog can please everyone. While it would be great if your Cocker delighted each judge she met, you should not count on this happening, for dogs of that caliber are extremely rare. It is much more important that your dog pleases you. Never blame your dog for failure in the ring, for if it were up to your Cocker, she would win every award possible to please you. So go to the shows. Have a good time, and learn all you can. Afterward, bring your beloved pet back home and show her that you still believe that she is the best dog in the world.

Conformation Events

Conformation events are shows in which the quality of the breeding stock is evaluated (so spayed or neutered dogs cannot compete in these events). In these shows, a Cocker would be judged on her appearance, physique, bearing, and temperament, and how well the dog conforms to the breed standard.

There are three types of conformation dog shows: all-breed shows, specialty shows for a specific breed, and group shows which are limited to dogs belonging to one of the seven AKC groups (Working, Herding, Sporting, Non-sporting, Hounds, Terrier, and Toy). Naturally, Cockers would compete in the sporting group. The AKC also offers children from 9 to 18 the

opportunity to compete in junior showmanship events. Here the juniors are judged on how well they present their dogs.

If you are interested and want to know more about conformation shows you can start by joining a local kennel club that will have information on training classes for the show ring. You should also attend a show as a visitor. If the grooming area is open to the public, talk to professional groomers to get some tips. If you are considering the purchase of a Cocker, you will have the benefit of many expert breeders and exhibitors to talk to. You can also find pet product vendors, and club booths that often offer helpful information. Once you know what to expect, you can better enjoy the experience of competitive dog shows.

Obedience Trials

There are three levels of training where a dog can compete for an obedience title: Novice, Open, and Utility. These trials are open to all registered dogs over the age of 6 months, that are qualified, by training, to participate.
✔ Novice class dogs usually have had at least one year of work at following practical commands used in everyday living such as "heeling" (both with and without a leash), "*come*," and "*stay*."
✔ Open level is more stringent, and includes exercises such as retrieving and jumping hurdles.
✔ The utility class is for the best of the best, and includes scent discrimination and silent signaling.
✔ Novice dogs compete to earn a Companion Dog (CD) title.
✔ Open class dogs compete for the Companion Dog Excellent (CDX) title. The top honor of Utility Dog (UD) is given to the best in the utility class.

The AKC also has six non-title classes that the beginning obedience handler and dog can enter to prepare for the titled ones. They are Pre-novice, Graduate Novice, Graduate Open, Brace, Veterinarians, and Versatility. Most competitors started by taking obedience classes as a way of gaining control over their pets, but found that working with their dogs can be a very rewarding experience. If you are interested in finding out more, a list of scheduled events is available from the AKC, as well as a copy of the AKC Obedience Regulations.

Hunting Tests and Field Trials

Working in the field with a Cocker is one of the greatest feelings a hunter can experience. Cockers are flushing spaniels, and their purpose in the field is to hunt, flush, and retrieve birds. Because they are specialized, there are separate field trials and hunting tests that were devised specifically for the flushing spaniels. The major difference between a field trial and a hunting test is that hunting tests are designed to see how well a dog performs her hunting duties against an established standardized platform, where a field trial provides competition in a dog versus dog venue. The AKC has published specific field trial rules and procedures, as well as regulations for AKC hunting tests specifically for spaniels, which you can find on their web site.

If you go to watch a trial, you will see one of the great spectacles of dog handling—a hunting dog and its master working in tandem, trying to perfect their synchronization. Always keep in mind that great dog work is the end result of excellent breeding, and a great deal of careful training.

Agility Trials

Agility competitions have become more and more popular each year. It is truly a sport for those energetic owners who want to have fun with their Cockers. Not only will it help create a lasting bond between the dog and trainer, it will also help to keep you both fit. In agility trials both the dog and handler need to run at full speed while having to perform exercises both accurately and safely.

Dogs can compete in either the AKC Standard Class, which includes obstacles such as climbing and descending an A-frame, traversing an elevated dog walk, and crossing a see-saw, or the AKC Jumpers with Weaves Class, which involve jumps, tunnels, and weave poles. Both classes offer increasing levels of difficulty as the dogs compete to earn a Novice, Open, Excellent, and Master title.

For those who have never seen an agility competition, I strongly urge you to attend one in your area, as the excitement that the top dog/handler teams can generate is unparalleled in the competition ring.

Paper Training

The objective of paper training is to get your puppy to urinate and defecate on newspapers spread out in an area of your choosing. Naturally you should choose an area that is easy to clean, such as a kitchen or bathroom. You must take care to make sure that the area you choose is not too close to your puppy's eating or sleeping areas, because your Cocker will instinctively try to keep those areas clean and will not excrete near them.

✔ Start by confining your puppy to the area you have chosen until she voids. If she used the paper, remove the top soiled sheet, and place fresh, clean papers under

You should start house-training your puppy as soon as possible. Be sure you have her total attention, and use hand gestures to help the puppy understand your verbal commands.

what were formerly the bottom sheets. By doing this you will be leaving the scent from the bottom papers exposed so that the puppy can relocate the area more easily to repeat the act.

✔ If the puppy misses the paper on her first attempt, get the scent of the dog's urine onto a sheet of newspaper and place it on top of the other sheets. Then thoroughly clean the area where the "accident" occurred. It is important to remove all scent from the inappropriate area that the puppy used so she will not become confused by finding her scent in two different locations the next time she has to relieve herself.

✔ Try to remember that after eating, drinking, playing, or waking up, your Cocker puppy will probably need to empty her bladder and bowels. Young puppies need to relieve themselves every few hours. Often, the only sign your puppy will give you is that she will begin sniffing the ground, searching for the right place to do her business. Some puppies may begin sniffing the ground and running around frantically, in which case you have only seconds to react. Pick up the puppy and place her on the newspaper in the designated area of your home. You can

then gently restrain the puppy's movements until she has relieved herself on the paper. Be sure to praise your puppy after she has "gone"on the paper.

Cage Training

Cage training offers a faster and easier alternative to paper training, as it takes advantage of your puppy's instincts to keep its sleeping area clean. If your puppy is wary on her first encounter with the cage, make the cage more appealing by placing some toys inside for your pet to play with. After you confine the puppy to her cage a few times with her excreta, she will quickly learn to restrain herself until you let her out of her cage. Naturally, you must take the puppy outdoors to relieve herself as soon as you let her out of the cage. Establish a time schedule for letting your Cocker out to relieve herself. As your trust in your puppy grows, and she becomes more used to the schedule, you can let her out of her cage for longer and longer periods of time. Eventually, you will be able to leave the cage door open at all times without fear of "accidents," provided that you take your puppy outside as scheduled.

Outdoor Training

Outdoor training begins when you first bring your puppy home. Before taking her indoors, take her for a walk in the area you have chosen for her elimination. Give your puppy plenty of time to do her business and be sure to praise her for a job well done. Verbal praise and petting will help build your puppy's confidence and will increase your chances of future successful performances.

Most puppies need to relieve themselves as many as six times a day, so you will need to take your puppy outdoors about once every three to four hours. It is also advisable to walk the puppy after each of her meals. When a puppy's stomach is full it will exert additional pressure on the bladder, so it is best not to wait too long. You should take your puppy for her last walk as late in the evening as possible. This will give you the greatest chance that your Cocker puppy will not suffer any accidents during the night. If you continue to bring your puppy to the same area each time, and praise her for each success, she will eventually seek out this area on her own.

Cleaning Up

It is true that canine droppings are aesthetically unpleasant, and it is your responsibility as a dog owner to clean them up. As these droppings can be considered a minor health hazard, many towns and cities have made it illegal not to clean up after your pet.

Wherever you walk your Cocker, carry a plastic bag or "pooper scooper" with you and dispose of the mess in its proper place. When cleaning your garden or yard, it is still best to pick up and dispose of the droppings in well-sealed plastic bags in a garbage can instead of burying them underground, as roundworms and tapeworms can be transmitted in the feces. For those "accidents" that happen in the home,

When training outdoors, do not forget that it is the responsibility of all dog owners to clean up after their pets. In some areas, the law requires them to do so.

clean with an odor-eliminating disinfectant. Do not use ammonia because the smell may remind your puppy of her urine.

Accidents Will Happen

No matter which method of house-training you choose, it is inevitable that "accidents" will eventually occur. If you discover that while you were asleep, your Cocker puppy could no longer control herself, remember that it was an accident. It will not do you or your puppy any good to get angry or to administer punishment. Puppies have very short memories, so if you do not catch them in the act, or make the discovery shortly afterward, a scolding will only confuse your pet. Should you catch her in the act, rebuke your puppy with a sharp "*No!*" and then put her in her cage. Never spank your puppy and *never, never, never* put your puppy's nose in the mess. Not only is this unsanitary, but it may upset the puppy to such an extent that you will have a second mess to clean up.

UNDERSTANDING COCKER SPANIELS

The Cocker Spaniel is an extremely complex creature. To understand his behavior patterns, we must take a close look at the process by which dogs evolved, became domesticated, and were selectively bred to create the pure breed we know today.

The Cocker Spaniel's Nature

Regardless of breed, all dogs can trace their ancestry to a form of wild dog or wolf. Wolves and wild dogs live in a highly structured society in which members must behave in certain ways so that the pack can function as a group and live in harmony. One of these behavior patterns is called "ranking order."

Ranking Order

Ranking order is a process by which the stronger and more experienced animals are placed at the top of the social ladder, whereas the younger and weaker ones are subordinate. In the pack, all dogs submit to one of higher authority. This system, in essence, prevents violent fights from occurring and helps the animals to hunt and coexist as a group, thereby ensuring survival of the species.

The behavior pattern of ranking order is actually instinctive and can be seen in all of our modern dogs. It is the fact that dogs still possess this trait that allows us to train them. During the training process, you, the master, are enforcing your dominance over your pet. Once your puppy understands his subordinate role, he will naturally attempt to follow your commands.

Scent Marking

Another instinctive behavior that our modern Cocker has inherited is "scent marking." While this trait is more important to males, it plays a role in any dog's life. As you walk your Cocker, he will attempt to mark several prominent spots, such as trees, fence posts, and telephone poles, with his urine to designate his territory. Likewise, your dog will use his nose to interpret other scent marks as made by friends or foes.

Other Behaviors

There are several other instinctive behaviors that Cocker Spaniels have inherited from their wild ancestors, including their sexual drives and a parent's inborn vigilance to protect his offspring. Like the wild wolves, a female Cocker in heat will excrete a strong scent to attract males, and after the birth of her puppies will keep them close and shield them from anything she considers dangerous.

All of these inherited behavior patterns have a common denominator: each plays an important role in the survival of the individual and the survival of the species. Survival is of paramount importance to wild dogs and is so strong an instinct that it has never been bred out of any of our modern breeds.

Effects of Domestication

While instinctive behaviors still play major roles in the lives of modern Cockers, as a result of domestication this breed has developed many new traits that are passed from one generation to the next. All of these qualities resulted from extensive contact with humans.

Once fearful of their two-legged competitors, some wild dogs eventually overcame their apprehension and developed a trust in people. With this came self-confidence. Also, through prolonged contact with humans, dogs were exposed to new experiences and learned new things. Specifically, through their history, the domesticated ancestors of the Cocker were exposed to the new experience of hunting with humans.

As one would expect, hunting dogs must undergo extensive training, and therefore they have a great deal of contact with their owners. After generations of this close relationship with humans, the Cocker has become a wonderful companion as well as a hunting aid. The merry, loyal, and obedient nature of the Cocker, as well as his physical characteristics, are the result of the careful, selective breeding practices of hunters and other enthusiasts. These breeders have likewise been responsible for weeding out

many of the inherent canine behaviors that would be undesirable in a hunting dog.

In summary, the nature of the Cocker Spaniel is a blend of two separate elements. The first includes all of the inherited behaviors that are the result of the strong survival instincts of the Cocker's wild ancestors. The second element consists of the selectively bred traits and characteristics that have evolved in this breed since the time when dogs were first domesticated. It is the combination of the inborn behavior patterns and the character traits acquired over long periods of time that has made the Cocker Spaniel a loyal hunting companion and one of the most popular dogs in the world.

How Dogs Communicate

In the preceding chapter we pointed out that dog trainers must use vocal tones and body gestures to get their ideas across to their students. It is just as important, however, for pet owners to be able to understand what their dogs are trying to tell them. Cockers will use their voices, body language, and facial expressions to convey their moods and emotions.

Forms of Communication

While the Cocker's primary form of vocal communication is barking, these dogs, like most other breeds, are capable of a variety of sounds, from a high-pitched whine to a deep growl. Because dogs rarely make noises without a reason, each individual sound or combination of sounds a Cocker makes has a specific purpose. A dog may yelp in fright or pain, whine and whimper when lonely or seeking attention, groan when content or ailing, and bark in

anger or glee. If you listen carefully and observe your dog's movements, you will soon learn the meanings of the various sounds.

Body language is an equally important indicator of your dog's mood. A joyous Cocker jumps up and down eagerly and may bark, or may roll over exposing his undersides in the hope of a good belly scratching. A dog that crouches and lowers his head to the floor is exhibiting fear, either of punishment, or of an intruder, or of another dog.

The best indicator of your dog's emotions, however, is his tail. A happy dog will wag his tail briskly. It is even possible to tell how happy your pet is by how much he wags his tail: the more wag, the happier the dog. Strangely enough, Cockers seem to know that their docked tails may not be adequate to tell the whole story, so they tend to wiggle their entire backsides to show how happy they are.

The tail is used to show other emotions as well. A frightened Cocker will point his tail straight down. An alert or attentive Cocker will raise his tail and hold it perfectly still, while a placidly content dog will hold his tail at a slightly lower angle and wag it slowly.

The contented spaniel may also choose to lie down in a sprawled-out manner, either on his side or on his belly with his head propped up on his paws. A Cocker will usually choose to take up this position in a location where he can keep an eye on his beloved master.

When the Cocker stretches himself out and tenses his body, this can mean several things. If the dog's neck hair also stands on end, consider this a warning of potential danger or anger. Sometimes this position is taken before a defensive stand or an attack. Should a sprawled-out, tense Cocker show a wagging or rotating tail, however, the dog is most likely in a joyous or playful mood. This is the type of position a Cocker may take before making a mock hunting spring toward his favorite toy.

The final indicator of your Cocker's moods is his facial expressions and gestures. This breed uses his eyes, ears, mouth, lips, and tongue to show a variety of feelings, from happiness to sadness, joy to anger, cockiness to disappointment, and alertness to mischievousness.

An alert or inquisitive dog will raise the upper portions of his ears, and an inquisitive dog may cock his head to one side and watch you with wide-open eyes. In a contented dog, the mouth is closed and the ears are in normal position. Cockers are capable of expressing many different emotions and will even smile when they are happy. A Cocker does this by opening his mouth slightly, sticking out the tip of his tongue, and pulling back on the corners of his lips to expose a portion of his teeth.

Cockers use their mouths and tongues for other purposes as well. A tired or hot dog will open his mouth wide, hang out his tongue, and pant in order to expel excess body heat. The Cocker will use his tongue to lick members of

---

TIP

When to Be Wary
Be wary of any dog that has his ears back, his upper lips raised, his mouth open, and the hairs on the back of his neck raised, and that is growling. Although you will rarely see a Cocker in this condition, remember that these are all warning signs of fear and/or anger, and that they may presage an attack.

---

his human family in an effort to express his love and devotion. While some people find "dog kisses" a little distasteful, you should never forget that this is how dogs show their closeness with members of their own kind.

The Cocker's Sense Organs
Dogs in general, and hunting dogs in particular, rely more on their senses of smell and hearing than they do on their other senses.

The Sense of Smell
Your Cocker's olfactory system, which governs his sense of smell, is more than 40 times more powerful than a human's, and he uses this system to a greater extent. A Cocker depends on his sense of smell to locate food, find a mate, interpret territorial boundaries, and track down prey during the hunt. Cockers can remember thousands of odors and have the ability to associate them with the proper people, places, and animals.

The Sense of Hearing
A Cocker's sense of hearing, his auditory system, is also superior to that of humans. Cockers can hear a wider range of sounds, including very high-pitched frequencies such as those emitted by "silent" dog whistles (Galton whistles). Cockers can also hear sounds at a greater distance than humans. Like their keen sense of smell, their acute hearing is important to their skill as hunting dogs, both for locating prey and for taking long-distance directions from their masters.

Cockers, like other breeds, also have the ability to differentiate and remember certain sounds. A friend tells me that she knows a few minutes in advance when her husband is coming home, for their Cocker becomes all excited at the impending arrival. The dog, it seems, is able to recognize the sound of the family car while it is quite a few blocks away.

The Sense of Vision

Although a Cocker's peripheral vision is greater than that of humans, these dogs cannot focus on an object as sharply. As a result, their eyes may not perceive an animal until it starts to move. The hunting Cocker, therefore, relies much more on smelling and hearing its prey than on spotting a still target.

Other Senses

While the Cocker Spaniel's coat offers the dog protection from the elements, as well as from thorns and thickets, it also results in a lack of body sensitivity. The body parts not covered by the dense coat, such as the nose and muzzle, however, have a much greater degree of feeling.

Like other dogs, the Cocker may possess other senses that we do not completely understand. Included in these is an innate sense of navigation. We have all heard stories of dogs, lost on vacations, that traveled hundreds of miles to return home. At the present time this phenomenon is being examined by researchers, but there is still no explanation.

In keeping with your Cocker's heritage as a hunting dog, it is important that your pet learn not to fear people or other animals with which he comes in contact. Although it is normal for your Cocker to be wary of strangers, the dog should never display fear. To help your Cocker learn how he should react, you need to introduce him to the outside world and the ways of humans while he is still very young. In addition

to eliminating fear, this exposure will help to instill the self-confidence that should be present in all Cockers. The following sections are designed to help you understand how your Cocker should react to different people and situations and what steps you can take to avoid trouble.

Life Cycle Changes

Emotional Growth

The first major change that your Cocker puppy will experience is when you remove him from his littermates at the tender age of seven or eight weeks. This marks the start of his emotional growth, since your puppy will begin to develop a new relationship with you. At this age puppies are very impressionable, as well as curious and mischievous. It is important to his emotional development that he learns the rules of your home, as well as being able to differentiate play from seriousness.

Even before you bring the new puppy home, he will have begun testing his strength through mock fights with his littermates. This not only helps his motor skills, it also acts as the first steps where each dog begins to learn his rank in the pack. As with human children, this is also a time when the puppy begins to test the limits of the rules through interactions with his mother.

When you first bring your puppy home he will be exceptionally adaptable, both emotionally and physically, and as a result can learn very rapidly. Unfortunately, he is just as capable of learning bad habits as he is good ones. It is, therefore, extremely important to begin training your puppy immediately.

How Old Is My Cocker?

Dog/Human Age Equivalents

Dog's Age	Human's Age	Dog's Age	Human's Age
2 months	14 months	7 years	49 years
3 months	3 years	8 years	56 years
6 months	6 years	9 years	63 years
8 months	10 years	10 years	65 years
12 months	17 years	11 years	71 years
18 months	21 years	12 years	75 years
2 years	25 years	13 years	80 years
3 years	30 years	14 years	84 years
4 years	36 years	15 years	87 years
5 years	40 years	16 years	89 years
6 years	42 years	17 years	95 years

By the time your puppy is 12 or 13 weeks old, he will have become completely aware of himself and his new home. His greatest joy will be to share his new discoveries with you, and he will begin to investigate everything in his environment. During this stage your puppy will begin to lose his baby teeth, which are replaced with permanent ones, so many of his investigations center around what objects taste like, and how hard they are to chew. Remember to have plenty of chew toys on hand to satisfy your puppy's urges. Keep in mind that the puppy is still very impressionable. Be sure to treat him with extra care, and consistently teach him the basic rules of your house, while maintaining control of your emotions.

Adolescence and Adulthood

At seven to ten months old, your puppy will be close to his full adult size. Curiosity will be replaced by bold, assertive interest. He is beginning to reach sexual maturity and will enter a stage that is the equivalent of human adolescence. He will have become very comfortable in his environment and with your lifestyle and will begin to feel that he should be included in all of your activities. If you have been adhering to your training regimen, your Cocker should know exactly what you expect from him and how he should behave. However, he will instinctively try to challenge you in order to improve his rank in your household. When this happens, remain in control and do not lose your temper. Just teach your dog, in a calm and firm manner, that you are in charge and are the leader of the pack. Doing this will lead your dog through its final stage of development.

Once a Cocker reaches maturity, at between 12 and 18 months of age, he will be fairly set in his ways and will probably not undergo any major behavioral changes (with the exception of mating urges). Your consistency, even temper, and ability to maintain control should now pay off in many years of companionship with a loving, trustworthy, and devoted Cocker Spaniel.

Cockers and Children

The Cocker Spaniel has always been hailed as a great lover of home and family, and under normal circumstances is completely trustworthy. This breed has been known to bond closely with children and at times may become extremely protective of them.

A Cocker will provide companionship, fun, and enjoyment for all children. A puppy that grows up with them considers himself one of the family. Your Cocker will teach your children the importance of affection and warmth, and serve as an example of absolute integrity, for he will never betray them. Cockers are the ultimate playmates because they love to run and frolic, especially with children.

It is important to remember, however, that the Cocker, although a very rugged and sturdy dog, is not a physical match for older, boisterous children. While a Cocker will normally not object to a little roughhouse play, he may take exception to having his ears, tail, or nose pinched, pushed, or pulled. Therefore, children must be taught how to treat their dog and must be careful to avoid all sensitive areas, especially the eyes. If you have a puppy, you should supervise all play sessions with the children until the dog is both large enough and strong enough for occasional rough handling.

Children should also be taught never to disturb a dog while he is eating or sleeping. Explain to them that, although their dog is a loving pet, he may nip if he is surprised or frightened.

You can ensure a lasting relationship between your Cocker and your children by

involving them in the responsibilities of dog care. Encourage them to participate in feeding, grooming, walking, and training the family pet.

Cockers and the New Baby

Reports of attacks on infants by family dogs have led some people to give up their devoted pets when a new baby arrives. This is truly a shame, for Cockers are at their best when they have children to play with. Moreover, animal behavior experts who have studied this problem have concluded that most dogs will not be aggressive toward infants. Dogs that are aggressive toward people, or that tend to chase and attack small animals, however, should never be left unsupervised with an infant.

Precautions

If you are expecting an addition to your household, there are several precautions you can take to make sure your Cocker will accept the new baby.

✔ Train the dog to sit or lie down for long periods of time before the baby is born. As you increase the time, accustom your dog to the activities it can expect to see once the baby arrives. Use a doll to imitate carrying, feeding, changing, and bathing the newborn. Remember to praise and reward your dog if he stays still and does not attempt to follow or interfere.

✔ After the birth of the infant, but before bringing him or her home, give your Cocker something the baby has used in the hospital, such as a blanket or towel, so that he can become familiar with the little one's scent. Upon returning from the hospital, have the mother greet the dog without the baby. Then place the baby in the nursery, and deny the dog access by using a screen door or folding gate. In this way the dog can see and hear the infant and get used to its presence before the two actually meet.

✔ When the meeting finally occurs, one person should control and praise the dog while another holds the baby. Have the dog sit, and show him the baby. They can remain together for as long as the dog stays calm. In the following weeks you can gradually increase the length of the dog's visit.

✔ While you should never allow the two to be together unsupervised, you must be sure to include your dog in as many activities involving the baby as possible. Your Cocker should never feel neglected. By exercising sensitivity to your pet's feelings, you will create an even stronger bond between your Cocker and your child.

Cockers and Other Pets

While Cockers usually get along well with other dogs, you should be careful not to let your pet play freely with smaller animals such as birds or hamsters. After all, the Cocker is a hunting dog. Cats, on the other hand, should be dealt with on an individual basis. I have seen Cockers and cats that got along like best friends, and I have seen some that were worst enemies.

Socialization

If you own two Cockers, they will enjoy each other's companionship, and you should rarely have trouble. Just remember to divide your attention between them evenly. If you do decide to get a second dog, be aware that you will need additional equipment, including another sleeping box or crate and other food dishes.

It is important that your puppy becomes acquainted with other dogs, and other people as well. Your Cocker must become used to crowds and the noises of traffic. Likewise, he must learn how to interact with others of his

own kind, a lesson that can be learned only if your precious pet is allowed to romp and play with other dogs. If you become overprotective of your Cocker and hardly ever let him off the leash, he will not have the freedom to meet and familiarize himself with other dogs and consequently may develop an almost neurotic attitude toward them. It is not at all strange for a Cocker to be wary of anything that makes his master anxious. As a result, a Cocker that is inexperienced in meeting other dogs may act abnormally when an encounter is forced upon him. In many cases this abnormal behavior confuses the other dog and may lead to biting or even vicious fighting.

Therefore, make it a habit to walk your Cocker in areas, such as a park, where he is bound to come into contact with other dogs. When you see another dog on lead approaching, restrain your Cocker, and ask the other dog owner if it is all right with him or her if the two dogs meet. If the other owner gives you permission, then you should both bring the two dogs together slowly. Once they are close, slacken the leash, as a dog that is kept on a tight lead tends to be a little bolder, knowing you are there, and may be more inclined to fight. Dog etiquette dictates that the two dogs sniff nose to nose. Once familiarity is established, each will then sniff the other's tail or rump. This action usually determines whether they will tolerate each other or become enemies.

In most cases, the two dogs will begin to wag their tails and show the ritualistic signs of friendship. Should you observe other signs, however, such as the hairs on the dogs' necks and backs standing on end, chances are that the animals will attempt to establish a ranking order and perhaps will even fight. At first each dog, in response to his instinct, will attempt to show dominance over the other, perhaps by trying to impress or intimidate the stranger. Dogs exhibiting intimidating behavior will attempt to make themselves look as large as possible by standing every hair on end, tensing their bodies, and taking an arrogant stance. Usually the contestant that achieves the larger appearance will win the higher ranking. If one dog lowers his head, tucks in his tail, and retreats, he has accepted the other dog as dominant and all will be well. If, however, neither backs down, then a growling exhibition or a fight may occur.

In most cases these fights look and sound much worse than they are. Ordinarily, as soon as one of the contestants turns his back and offers an unprotected throat to the other, the fight will end, for along with the instinct to establish ranking order, dogs are equipped with a hereditary behavior pattern that prevents them from biting a dog that acts submissively. Be warned, however, that dogs with behavior problems caused by poor breeding practices may not adhere to the rules of etiquette and may attempt to continue fighting and biting a dog that has shown submission.

If the dogs continue to fight, then you will need to separate them by pulling on the leash. Never try to physically separate fighting dogs, for you can be easily bitten. Sometimes you can get them to stop fighting by distracting them with jumping, yelling, or clapping your hands. Once the dogs are separated, remove your Cocker to a safer area.

Should the approaching dog be ownerless, you need to think twice before introducing them. While a stray dog may be someone's lost beloved pet, he may also be a dog that is fearful, has been neglected, or may have physical or behavioral problems. If you are unsure in

The Cocker and Its Master

Although owning a Cocker Spaniel is a responsibility that entails work, time, and energy, it is also a life-enriching experience. If you provide your Cocker with the training he needs and maintain his health and appearance, you will be rewarded many times over with companionship, fun, loyalty, and devotion. The work, time, and energy you put into raising the best dog possible will result in a healthy, long-standing relationship between you and your faithful companion.

But dogs are more than valued companions, hunters, and friends. They inhabit a place deep within us. They occupy our dreams and stimulate our imaginations. Your Cocker will fulfill some of your strongest psychic and spiritual needs. Researchers have only begun to examine the psychological benefits of owning and caring for a pet. Companion animals have been shown to reduce stress in their masters and are now being used for their therapeutic effect on the elderly, as well as the physically and mentally handicapped. The simplicity of a dog's behavior can keep us in touch with reality. Dogs are warm, affectionate, and extremely stable—never complex or capricious. They can help people overcome anxiety, grief, depression, loneliness, and pain.

In truth, the Cocker can play an important role in the lives of people of any background, status, or lifestyle. The dog will give you, his master, the unconditional love that you need. The long-term commitment you make to your pet will be rewarded by the emotional security of knowing that, no matter how bad a day you have had, when you eventually return home, your Cocker will make you feel loved and appreciated.

any way of the approaching dog's actions or body gestures, you should calmly remove your Cocker, and yourself, to a safe location, and call the local animal control department. If you are confident that the stray is not posing any threat, or displaying signs of being frightened, then you should still approach him with caution. You can then try to confine the dog in a safe, warm, and dry place and offer him food and water. If the dog has a tag, you can then contact his owner and make arrangements for the dog's safe return. If no identification tag can be found, notify the local animal control department who can come to get the dog and make sure he receives the proper medical attention and food that he may need.

Clubs

The American Spaniel Club, Inc.
www.asc-cockerspaniel.org
Kathleen L. Patterson
ASC Secretary
P.O. Box 4194
Frankfort, KY 40604-4194
asc.secretary@gmail.com

American Kennel Club
www.akc.org

American Cocker Spaniel Club of Canada
www.acscc.ca

Canadian Kennel Club
www.ckc.ca

The American Cocker Spaniel Club
   of Great Britain
www.acscgb.com

Poison Control

Animal Poison Control Center
(888)-426-4435
www.aspca.org

Health Registries

The Canine Health Foundation
www.akcchf.org

Canine Eye Registration Foundation (CERF)
www.vmdb.org/cerf.html

Orthopedic Foundation for Animals (OFA)
www.offa.org

Canine Health Information Center (CHIC)
www.caninehealthinfo.org

Rescue Groups

The American Spaniel Club, Inc.
www.asc-cockerspaniel.orgg/index/php/
rescue.html
Heidi Braun, ASC & ASCF Rescue Chair
N79W12846 Fond du Lac Avenue
Menomonee Falls, WI 53051

Cocker Spaniel Rescue of New England, Inc.
www.csrne.org

Cocker Spaniel Rescue of East Texas
www.cockerkids.org

Florida Cocker Spaniel Rescue
www.floridacocker.org

CSRBC Cocker Spaniel Rescue
(British Columbia)
www.csrbc.org

Books

Dr. Alvin Grossman. *The American Cocker Spaniel.* San Jose, CA: Doral Publishing, Inc., 1988.

D. Caroline Coile, Ph.D. *The Cocker Spaniel Handbook.* Hauppauge, NY: Barron's Educational Series, Inc., 2007.

Norman Austin & Jean Austin. *The Complete American Cocker Spaniel.* New York, NY: Hungry Minds, Inc., 1993.

J. C. Barnes. *Living with a Sporting Spaniel.* Hauppauge, NY: Barron's Educational Series, Inc., 2005.

About the Author

Jaime J. Sucher is Director of Research and Development for a manufacturer of pet products. He is the author of *Golden Retrievers, Shetland Sheepdogs,* and numerous articles on pet nutrition.

Photo Credits

Cheryl Ertelt: 33; Isabelle Francais: 4, 7, 8, 11, 14, 17, 22, 40, 44, 45, 46, 49, 59, 62, 67, 75, 79, 82, 85, 89, and 92; and Pets by Paulette: 2-3, 5, 12, 13, 18, 21, 23, 24, 26, 27, 28, 29, 30, 31, 35, 36, 37, 41, 42, 43, 47, 53, 56, 68, 69, 76, 83, and 90.

Cover Photos

Front cover, back cover, inside front cover, inside back cover: Shutterstock.

All inquiries should be addressed to:
Barron's Educational Series, Inc.
250 Wireless Boulevard
Hauppauge, NY 11788
www.barronseduc.com

Library of Congress Catalog Card No. 2008039157

ISBN-13: 978-0-7641-4101-0
ISBN-10: 0-7641-4101-5

Library of Congress Cataloging-in-Publication Data
Sucher, Jaime J.
    Cocker spaniels : everything about purchase, care, nutrition, behavior, and training / Jaime J. Sucher ; full-color photographs illustrations by Michele Earle-Bridges.
        p. cm. — (A complete pet owner's manual)
    Includes index.
    ISBN-13: 978-0-7641-4101-0
    ISBN-10: 0-7641-4101-5
    1. Cocker spaniels. I. Earle-Bridges, Michele, ill. II. Title.

SF429.C55S83 2009
636.752'4—dc22   2008039157

Printed in China
9 8 7 6 5 4 3 2 1

Important Note

This book is concerned with selecting, keeping, and raising Cocker Spaniels. The publisher and the author think it is important to point out that the advice and information for Cocker Spaniel maintenance applies to healthy, normally developed animals. Anyone who acquires an adult dog or one from an animal shelter must consider that the animal may have behavioral problems and may, for example, bite without any visible provocation. Such anxiety-biters are dangerous for the owner as well as the general public.

Caution is further advised in the association of children with dogs, in meetings with other dogs, and in exercising the dog without a leash.